Preface 5

Summary 8

1.1 .1 PERFORATED CARDS 9

1.1.2 THE FIRST COMPUTER.................................10

1.1.3 THE FIRSTTRANSISTORS 12

1.1.4 MICRO-COMPUTING 14

2 THE MICRO PROCESSORAND THE PERIPHERALS 16

Historical 19

2.1 THE ERA OF MULTIMEDIAAND DIGITAL 60

With the microcomputer,computers are 60

2.2 HOW IS INTERNET BORN? 62

2.2.3 WHAT IS WORLD WIDE WEB? 64

2.2.4 HOW CAN WE SUBMIT MESSAGES ON THE INTERNET? 66

3.3.1 HOW TO TRANSPORT ACODED INFORMATION IN THE..69

3.3.2 From the bell to the telegram.....................70

3.3.3 THE "FATHERS" OF THETELEPHONE 72

3.3.4 THE PRINCIPLE AND COMPONENTS OF PHONE 76

4 ENSURING THE THREAD 83

Context : 86

4.4.2 OBJECT OF THE CONTRIBUTION 88

4.4.3 THEORETICALFRAMEWORK 89

4.4.4 INTRODUCTION 90

5 THE CONCEPT 98

5.5.3 TENACIOUS OBSTACLESTHAT OPPOSE A ADMISSION OF ICT ASFACTORS DEVELOPMENT IN AFRICA 101

5.5.4 THE ARGUMENT OF LUXURY IMPRODUCTIVE THAT CONSTITUTE ICT INRELATION TO NUMEROUS PRIORITIES FORDEVELOPMENT IN AFRICA 103

5.5.5 THE SPECIAL DIFFICULTY TO MEASURE THE ECONOMIC AND SOCIAL WEIGHT OF ICT IN DEVELOPMENT. A REALOBSTACLE BUT 110

6. THE CHANGE OF PARADIGM IMPOSES ONE POSITIVE VISION OF THEROLE OF ICT IN THE DEVELOPMENT 116

6.6.1 ICT IS ACTUALLYINSTRUMENTS AT THE SERVICE OF DEVELOPMENT IN AFRICA 123

6.6.2 LIMITATIONS OF THE ACCOUNTING APPROACH 123

6.6.2 THE STRUCTURING ORFACTOR FACTOR INDIRECT: A MORE OPERATIVE INDICATOR ASSESSING THE ROLE OF ICT IN THE

DEVELOPMENT 130

6.6.3 RECOMMENDATIONSFOR SUCCEEDING IMPLEMENTATION OF APROJECT 142

7. CASE STUDIES 142

7.1 INTRODUCTION 142

7.7.2 CHOICE OF INNOVATIVETECHNOLOGIES .. 148

7.7.3 MOBILE TELEPHONYAND APPLICATIONS 151

7.7.4 TECHNOLOGIESWIRELESS 160

7.7.5 BUSINESS MODELS ANDPOSSIBILITIES 167

OF COMMUNITY ICTPROJECTS 167

7.7.6 Community PropertyModels and Directed Models by the communities 168

8. COOPERATIVES 175

8.8.1 MODELS DIRECTED BYTHE GOVERNMENT 178

8.8.2 MUNICIPAL BROADBAND NETWORKS ... 179

8.8.3 PROVISION OF SERVICES TO COMMUNITIES 181

8.8.4 PRIVATE SECTORMODELS AND CREATION OF COMMUNITYUNDERTAKINGS 185

9. RECOMMENDATIONS FORSUCCEEDING IMPLEMENTATION OF APROJECT 190

9.9.1 CAS^2 E STUDIES 198

9.9 .2CONCLUSION 206

ABBREVIATIONS ANDACRONYMS 234

Bibliography References cited 244

Preface

Enamelled observation, thisbook examines with a logic of the emergence of Information Technology and the ICT telecommunication and itsimpact on the continent. News is teeming with these ideas and projects that occupythe front of the stage, fuel thedebate before disappearing without warn to pop up a few monthsor years later without the situation having changed. Information Technologyand Telecommunication "ICT" feeds its own "snakes of sea ". So, who has not heard athousand times. Experts and managers policies evoke the establishment of a far-reachingplan

to computerize all urban andrural communes. In the

same spirit, the best informed people predict us

regularly the next emergence TV centers. But, each time, the soufflé falls, leaving users alone in the face of theseICT tools. Certainly, the last progress allows the most courageous to dispense with the support paper, e-mail, teleconference,archiving, fax, from the PC ... everything is technically possible. But who has really want to try to set uptools, materials and software, which is essential for setting up an "office virtual "not a lot of people intruth. That's why we have decided to offer you a practical work dedicated to TV centers in Mali. In all its facets.

The presentation of a material, a document reflects the attention and importance of hisdesigner, as well as his professionalism. It then becomes entirely appropriate, for ICT professionals to insist onthe application of rudiments relating to the presentation ofa professional job, of course, the realization of this document necessitated choices among the suggestions made by computerand electronics colleagues for example, for the submission of a brief, and otherrules must be respected, wheneverwe are convinced that readers willhave fundamental knowledge in computer science and anotion in electronics that is essentially the focal point of ICT.

Summary

This article focuses on the sudden appearance of new user sin Internet access points. The development of the technologiesof information and communication has aroused, areal enthusiasm at local populations. Despite theweak and the d penetration of the internet at Mali, there is an unprecedented appropriation ofsocial networks and the creation of information platforms to enable both others to express. Recent events in Mali including the coupd'etat Military against President Amadou Toumani Toure pushed users to attend TV centers and cybercafés. This emergence is also characterized by the online posting of real-time information on all *the* activities on the countryon the inside or out is.

1.1 .1 PERFORATED CARDS

Around 1800, the FrenchmanJoseph-Marie Jacquard puts point a loom that uses cartonsperforated to control the movements ofneedles. A little later, in 1833, theEnglish Charles Babbage take this principle back andbuild a machine again more elaborate than the calculating machines of the time:

his is capable of performing allthe operations and store the results. It is to hispartner, the mathematician **Ada Byron**, that we owe a little more late the basic principles ofprogramming. In 1890, the American Hermann Hollerith uses a similar device to strip theresults of the US census. His company,Tabulating Machine Company, will later becomeIBM.

1.1.2 THE FIRST COMPUTER

In 1945, in the United States, isborn the ENIAC (Electronic Numerator Integrator andComputer), the first real computer of history. Itdiffers from all the previous machines for two reasons:

- First, it is an electronic machine. There has more mechanical workings; the information is transported by electrons, charged particles electricity, which move very fast;

- moreover, it is a programmable machine . it

means that we can record instructions that will run without human intervention.

This computer is very impressive: it weighs 30 tons and occupies an area of about 100m². To do it operate, more than 17,000 vacuum tubes are required. Sometimes cockroaches break into these tubes, distorting the results. It's for this reason we still talk today about" bug computing ". This word comes from the English bug , which means "cockroach"

1.1.3 THE FIRST TRANSISTORS

After the Second World War, the circuits electronic devices are still mere lamps. In 1948, the invention of the transistor , a very compact circuit who does not fear shocks and does not heat, will accelerate the development ofcomputers. The need for computer programsincrease and new professions appear: programmer, analyst, system engineer.

The software industry is emerging little by little. In the1950s, the first advanced languages appear: Cobol and Fortran , forexample, make computers much easier to program.

1.1.4 MICRO-COMPUTING

In 1964, integrated circuits(often called chips) are silicon-based , a very abundant in nature and which favors the miniaturization of electroniccomponents . This reduces the size and price of computers.

In 1971, the first microprocessor (Intel 4004) comes out of the workshops ofthe American company Intel . he contains 2,300 transistors and runs 60,000 instructions per second. In comparison, a modern microprocessor likethe Intel Pentium 4 includes tens of millions of transistors and executes several billioninstructions per second.

In 1981, IBM launched the PC(for Personal Computer , whichmeans "personal computer"). The PC revolutionizes the micro-computer because itis a computer compatible , that is, all writtensoftware for this machine work withanother PC computer, regardless of itsbrand and date of manufacturing. Many application software (word processing, databasemanagement, etc.) are readily available, including those from the Microsoft company of BillGates , founded in 1975. In 1984, Macintosh systemsfrom Apple Computer are the first to have an inter face graph : instead of having totype commands tedious keyboard, the user cannow serve as a mouse and click onicons . The first version of Windows,marketed by Microsoft in 1985, is inspiredby it to make use more friendly PCs. In the late 1980s, the firstcomputers laptops are emerging. They are lighter and less cumbersome than what isnow called opposition to "desktops" andpresent the advantage of beingtransported easily.

2 THE MICRO PROCESSORAND THE PERIPHERALS

Definition:

Until the early 1970s, thedifferent components electronic forming a processorcould not fit on a integrated circuit, which necessitated the interconnectionof many component including several integrated circuits. In 1971, society American Intel succeeds, forthe first time, in placing all components that constitute a processor on a single integratedcircuit

giving birth to the microprocessor[1]. This miniaturization allowed: to increase speeds[2] operation of the processors, thanks reducing distances between components; reduce costs by replacing multiple circuits with only one; to increase reliability: by removing connections between components of the processor, we delete one of the main vectors breakdown; to create much smaller computers: microcomputers ; to reduce energyconsumption[3]. The main features of a microprocessor are: The instruction set he can execute. here are some examples instructions that can be executed by a microprocessor: add two numbers, compare two numbers to determine if they are equal, pace of the microprocessor work. More clock speed increases, the more the microprocessor performs instructions in a second. All this is theoretical, in practice, according to the architecture of the processor, the number of clockcycles to achieve a elementary operation can varyfrom one cycle to several tens by execution unit (typically one on a conventional processor). For example, a 400 MHzprocessor A may be more faster than another B clocked at 1GHz, it all depends on their respective architectures. The combination of the preceding features determines the power of the microprocessor. The power of a microprocessor is expressed in Millions of Instructions Per Second (MIPS).In the the 1970s, microprocessors were making less than a million of instructions per second, the current processors (in 2007) can perform more than 10 billion instructions per second.

Historical

In 1969, the microprocessor was invented by two engineers from Intel : **Marcian H** off(nicknamed Ted Hoff) and **Federico Faggin**. **Marcian H** off formulated the architecture of the microprocessor (a block architecture and a set ofinstructions). The first

microprocessor marketed, on November 15, 1971, is the Intel 4004 4-bit, followed by the Intel 8008. It was originally usedto manufacture graphic controllers in text mode. Judged too slow by the customer who had asked forthe design, he became a processor of general use. These processors are the precursors of Intel 8080 , **ZilogZ80**, and of the future Intel x86 family. **O Federico Faggin** is the authora new design methodology for the chip and the Logic, founded for the firsttime on Silicon Technology developed by him in 1968 at Fairchild. He also led the design of the first microprocessor until its introduction on

the market in 1971.[Ref. necessary] In the 1970s, the concepts of datagram and of distributed computing , with ARPANET, the Cyclades and the network Distributed System Architecture , which in 1978became the "OSI-DSA ". The microprocessor isquickly welcomed like stone angle of this distributed computing because it allows for decentralize computing, with less expensive machines and less bulky in the face of the monopoly IBM, produced in larger series. In 1990, **Gilbert Hyatt** claimed the paternity of the microprocessor based on apatent he had filed in 1970. The recognition of theprior art of the Hyatt patent allowed him to claim royaltieson all microprocessors manufactured around the world. However, the patent of Hyatt was invalidated in 1995 by the US Patent Office, on the basis that the microprocessor described in the application for patent had not been realized, nor could it have been the technology available at the time of filing the patent.

[Ref. necessary] The following table describes the main characteristics

of the microprocessors manufactured by Intel, and shows them fast and systematic evolution both in increasing the number of

transistors, in miniaturization of circuits, and in increasing power. It should be kept in mind that if this table describes the evolution of Intel's products, the evolution of the products of competitors followed withmore or less advance or late same walk. A computer program is, in essence, a flow of instructions

executed by a processor. Each instruction requires one to several clock cycles, the instruction is executed in asmany steps than necessary cycles. Microprocessors

sequencers execute the following statement when theyare done the current instruction. In thecase of parallelism of instructions, the microprocessor can handle several instructions in the same clock cycle, provided that thesedifferent instructions do not not simultaneously mobilize asingle internal resource.

In other words, the processor executes instructions that follow each other, and are not dependent on eachother at different stages completion. This upcoming runqueue is called a pipeline.

This mechanism was implemented the first time inyears 1960 by IBM. More advancedprocessors perform at the sametime time as many instructions asthey have pipelines, this to thecondition that all the instructions to beexecuted in parallel are not

interdependent, that is, theresult of the execution of

each of them does not modifythe conditions of one of the others. Processors ofthis type are called superscalar processors . Thefirst computer to be equipped with this type of processor was theSeymour **Cray CDC** 6600 in 1965.The Pentium is the first of thesuperscalar processors for PC compatible .Processor designers are notjust looking to execute   multiple independent instructions at the same time they

seek to optimize the executiontime of all instructions. For example the processor can sort the instructions of so that all its pipelines contain instructions independent. This mechanismis called out-of-order execution .

This type of processor has become essential for consumer

Machines in from the 1980s until the 1990s[5]. example

canonical of this type ofpipeline is that of a RISC processor , in five steps. The Intel Pentium 4has 35 stages of pipeline[6]. An optimized compiler for thiskind of processor will provide a code that will run faster. To avoid a loss of time related to waiting for news instructions, and especially thetime to reload the context between every thread change , thesmelters[7] have added to their processors optimization processes for that threads can share pipelines, caches andrecords. These processes, grouped under thename Simultaneous Multi-Threading, were developed inthe 1950s. to get an increase in performance, the compilers must take into account theseprocesses, it is necessary to recompile the programs for these types ofprocessors. Intel started to produce, in the early 2000s , processors implementing the

two-way SMT technology. These processors, the Pentium 4,

can simultaneously run two threads

that share the

same pipelines, caches andregisters. Intel called this

two-way SMT technology : the Hyper threading. The Super-As for threading, it is an SMTtechnology in which multiple threads also share thesame resources, but these Threads only run one after another and not simultaneously. For a long time already existedthe idea of coexisting processors within the same component, for example System on Chip. This included, for example, adding to the processor a arithmetic coprocessor , a DSP,or even a memory cache, possibly even all the components that are found on a motherboard. Processorsusing two or four cores appeared, like IBM's POWER4released in 2001. They have the technologies mentioned before. Computersthat have this type of processorscost less than buying of an equivalent number of processors, however, the performance are not directly comparable, itdepends on the problem treaty. Specialized APIs havebeen developed to leverage at the best of these technologies, like the ThreadingBuilding Blocks Intel.

Here is a list of microprocessors, with the manufacturers, the computers in which they were used, and their frequencies of use:

Intel (before 8088)

4004: 4-bit CISC

4040: 4-bit CISC

8008: 8-bit CISC

8080: 8-bit CISC

8085: 8-bit CISC

Zilog Z80: 8-bit CISC (the most common 8-bit processor in the world for its entire life, responsible for many personal computers in the 1980s, such as Sinclair machines, Amstrad CPC and PCW, game consoles Sega Master System...).

Zilog Z8000: family of 16-bit microprocessors composed of the z8001 (capable of addressing 8 MB of memory and the z8002 (64 KB)) - incompatible with the Z80.

Zilog Z80000: 32 bits - incompatible with the previous ones.

<u>6800 family</u>: 8-bit CISC 6800

6803 (present in Alice microcomputers sold at the time (1980s) by Matra & Hachette)

6809 (present on computers from the 1980s marketed by Thomson and equipping schools in France: MO5, MO6, TO7, TO8, etc.)

6502 family (MOS Technology created by Chuck Peddle, second source: Western Design Center): 8-bit CISC (first inexpensive processor (at launch around US$5 compared to US$25 for competitors)).

6502 (processor of the Apple II, Vic20, Commodore 64, and many other machines, including washing machines...)

6507

6509

6510

8501

65c816 (16-bit processor of the Apple IIgs and Super Nintendo)

Motorola 68000 family

68000: 16-32 bits CISC (processor of the first Apple Macintosh, Amiga, Atari ST, Mega Drive and SNK Neo-Geo game consoles...). It was very popular in the late 80s and considered easier to program than the Intel x86.

68008: 8-32 bit CISC

68010: 16-32 bit CISC

68020: 32-bit CISC

68030: 32-bit CISC

68040: 32-bit CISC

68060: 32-bit CISC

ColdFire: 16-bit CISC

DragonBall: 16-bit CISC (Palm)

88000 family (Motorola): 32-bit RISC

88100

<u>Intel RISC family</u>: 32-bit RISC

i860 (had little success, probably in part due to internal competition produced by the i960)

i960 (had few applications visible to the general public; but very present in military markets and graphics functions and high-end printers)

x86 family (Intel and others). The PC processor family.

8086 (clones manufactured by NEC):

16-bit CISC

8088: 8-16 bits CISC (the processor of the IBM PC).

80186: 16-bit CISC

80188: 8-16 bits CISC

80286: 16 CISC bits (16 data bits, 20 address bits (up to 64 K segments of 64 KB maximum size.))

80386 (clones made by AMD and Cyrix): 32-bit CISC

80486 (clones made by AMD, Cyrix, UMC and others) 32-bit CISC

Pentium: 32-bit CISC

Pentium MMX: 32-bit CISC

Pentium Pro: 32-bit CISC

Pentium II: 32-bit CISC

Pentium III: 32-bit CISC

Pentium 4: 32-bit and 64-bit CISC

Pentium D: 32 and 64 bit CISC dual core

Pentium M: 32-bit CISC

Celeron: 32-bit CISC

Xeon: 32 bits and 64 bits (since June 28, 2004) CISC

Core: 32-bit CISC

Core 2: 64-bit CISC

Core i7: 64-bit CISC

AMD K5: 32-bit CISC

AMD K6: 32-bit CISC

Athlon: 32-bit CISC

Duron: 32-bit CISC

Sempron: 32-bit CISC

Sempron 64: 32 and 64 bit CISC

Athlon 64: 32 and 64 bit CISC

Athlon 64 X2: 32 and 64 bits CISC dual core

Opteron: 32 and 64 bit CISC

Turion: 32 and 64 bits CISC`

Haipad: 32 and 64 bit CISC

Itanium family (Intel): 64 bits. Intended, according to Intel, to replace the x86 family with which it is incompatible, it is for the moment confined to high-end servers and stations. Its success seems mixed.

Itanium

Itanium 2

Crusoe family (Transmeta): VLIW (Very long instruction word) hardware architecture + (code morphing engine)

Crusoe 128-bit

Efficeon 256-bit

<u>POWER family (IBM)</u>: 32 and 64 bits RISC. Used in IBM calculators, graphics workstations, Unix servers, mainframes and minicomputers.

POWER1

POWER2

POWER3

POWER4

POWER4+

POWER5

POWER5+

POWER6

POWER7

PowerPC family (IBM and Motorola): 32 and 64 bits RISC. Used in IBM calculators, graphics workstations, Unix servers, mainframes and minicomputers, as well as in Macintoshes and the Nintendo GameCube console.

PowerPC 403

PowerPC 405

PowerPC 440

PowerPC 601

PowerPC 603

PowerPC 603e

PowerPC 604

PowerPC 604e

PowerPC 620 (64 bit)

PowerPC 750 (or G3)

PowerPC 7400-7450-7455 (or G4)

PowerPC 970 (or G5) (64 bit)

SPARC family (Sun Microsystems): 32 and 64 bit RISC. Used in Sun's calculators, graphics workstations and Unix servers.

Sun Sparc: 32-bit RISC

SuperSPARC: 32-bit RISC

MicroSparc: 32-bit RISC

HyperSPARC: 32-bit RISC

UltraSPARC I: 64-bit RISC

UltraSPARC IIi: 64-bit RISC

UltraSPARC III: 64-bit RISC

UltraSparc IV: 64-bit RISC, multi-stream, dual core

UltraSparc T1: 64-bit RISC, multi-stream, octa core

UltraSPARC T2: 64-bit RISC, multi-stream, octa core, 64 threads

LEON 32-bit RISC, free under GPL2,GPL3 license

ARM family (ARM Ltd., Intel and Texas Instruments). Used in PDAs of various brands, most often running PocketPC, as well as mobile phones and Acorn's RISC PC and Archimedes computers.

ARM7

ARM9 (Like OMAP from Texas Instruments)

ARM10

ARM11 (Like OMAP 2 from Texas Instruments)

StrongARM (Intel)

XScale (Intel)

Cortex-A8 (Like Texas Instruments OMAP3 or Freescale i.MX515)

Cortex-A9 (Like Texas Instruments OMAP4)

Mips family (Mips, NEC clones): 32 and 64 bit RISC used in Unix stations from SGI (Silicon Graphics Inc.) and Nintendo

R2000: 32-bit RISC, 12 to 33 MHz

R3000: 32-bit RISC, 20 to 40 MHz (SGI PlayStation)

R4000: 64-bit RISC, 50 to 250 MHz (Nintendo 64)

R4400: 64-bit RISC, 50 to 250 MHz

R5000: 64-bit RISC, 150 to 200 MHz

R5900: 64-bit RISC (PlayStation 2)

R6000: 64-bit RISC

R8000: 64-bit RISC, 75 to 90 MHz, multi-chip CPU, first MIPS superscalar

R10000: 64-bit RISC, 175 to 300 MHz

R12000: 64-bit RISC, 300 to 400 MHz

R14000: 64-bit RISC, 500 to 800 MHz

R16000: 64-bit RISC

R20000: 64-bit RISC

DEC Alpha family (DEC, then Compaq, then Hewlett-Packard): 64-bit RISC

Alpha 21064: 64-bit RISC, 150 to 300 MHz

Alpha 21164: 64-bit RISC, 300 to 433

MHz

Alpha 21264: 64-bit RISC, 500 MHz to 1.25 GHz

Alpha 21364: 64-bit RISC, 1 to 1.3 GHz

PA family (Hewlett-Packard): 32 (7000 series) and 64 bit (8000 series) RISC

PA 8000

PA 8200

PA 8500

PA 8700

PA 8800 dual core

PA 8900 dual core

SuperH family (Hitachi): 32-bit RISC

SH1

SH2 (Sega Saturn and Sega 32X console)

SH3

SH4 (Sega Dreamcast console)

MCore family (Freescale): 32-bit RISC

MMC2001

MMC2003

MMC2107

MMC2113

MMC2114

Name : the name of the microprocessor.

Number of transistors : the number of transistors containedin the microprocessor.

Engraving fineness (nm) : the diameter (in nanometers) of the most small wire connecting two components of the microprocessor. In comparison, the thickness of a human hair is 100 microns = 100,000 nm. The diameter of a silicon atom is of the order of 100 µm = 0.1 nm. Arriving in 2014 at the engraving finesse of the order of 10 nm, this diameter falls below 100 atoms of silicon. By increasing the fineness of engraving, we are getting closer to limits below which the electrical behavior of materials less and less of classical physics, but more and more more than quantum mechanics Clock **frequency**: the frequencyof the internal clock signal which speeds the microprocessor. MHz = million (s) of cycles per second. GHz = billion cyclesper second. Data Width : The first numberindicates the number of bits on which an operation is made.The second number indicates thenumber of bits transferred at a time between the memory and the microprocessor.

MIPS : the number of millionsof instructions made by the microprocessor in one second. Intel Core 2 Duomicroprocessor. Microprocessors are usuallygrouped into families, function of the instruction setthey execute. If this game of instructions often includes a common basis for the entire family, the most recent microprocessors in a family can submit new instructions. Thebackward compatibility in a family is not always assured. For example a program says x86 compatiblewritten for an Intel **80386** processor,

that allows memory protection, might not work on

previous processors, butworks on all processors

newer ones (for example anIntel Core Duo or an **Athlon AMD).** There are dozens of microprocessor families. Of those which have been used themost, we can **mention**: The family best known by thegeneral public is the x86 family , appeared in the late 1970s .developed mainly by companies Intel (Pentium manufacturer), AMD (manufacturer the Athlon), VIA and Transmeta. The first twocompanies dominate the market and theymanufacture most of the microprocessors for PC compatible microcomputers, and Macintosh since 2006. The MOS Technology 6502 thatwas used to make the Apple II, Commodore PET, whosedescendants served at the Commodore 64 and the Atari 2600 consoles. The MOS Technology6502 was made by former Motorola engineersand was very much inspired by Motorola 6800 .

The Zilog Z80 microprocessorhas been widely used in

1980s in the design of the first microcomputers

personal 8 bits like the TRS-80, the Sinclair ZX80, ZX81,

ZX Spectrum, the MSX standard, the Amstrad CPCs and later inembedded systems. The Motorola 68000 family

(also called m68k) from Motorola

animated the first Macintosh,Mega Drive, Atari ST and

Commodore Amiga . Theirderivatives (Dragonball, Cold Fire) are always used in embeddedsystems.

PowerPC microprocessorsfrom IBM and Motorola were until 2006 Macintosh microcomputers (manufacturedby Apple) . These microprocessors are also used in servers **IBM** P Series and various embedded systems . In the field of gaming consoles,

derivatives microprocessorsPowerPC equips Wii

(Broadway), GameCube (Gekko), Xbox 360 (three-core derivative named Xenon). The PlayStation 3is equipped with the Cell microprocessor , derived fromthe

POWER4, a architecture close to PowerPC. The MIPS architecture processors animated the work of Silicon Graphics, gameconsoles like the P Sone, the

Nintendo 64 and embeddedsystems, as well as

Routers Cisco . It is the first family to propose an architecture 64 bits with the MIPS R4000 in1991. The processors of the founder Chinese Loongson, are a newgeneration based on MIPS technologies, used in supercomputers and low power computers.

The ARM family is nowadaysonly used in

embedded systems, includingmany PDAs and smartphones. She has previously been used byAcorn for his

Archimedes and RiscPC . Speed of execution ofinstructions Frequency of operation The microprocessors are clocked by a clock signal (signal regular oscillation imposing a rhythm on the circuit). In themiddle of 1980s, this signal had a frequency of 4 to 8 MHz. In the 2000, this frequency reaches 4GHz. More this frequency is the higher the microprocessorcan run at a high rate basic instructions forprograms.

The increase in frequency has drawbacks: the higher it   is, the more power the processor consumes,and the more it heats: this implieshaving a solution of cooling of the adaptedprocessor; the frequency is notably limited by the switching times of logic gates : it is necessary between two "shots clock, digital signals have hadtime to travel all the path necessary to execute the expected instruction;for speed up treatment, you haveto act on many parameters

(size of a transistor , electromagnetic interactionsbetween circuits, etc.) it is becoming increasingly difficult to improve(all ensuring the reliability of operations).Overclocking The overclocking comprisesapplying to a microprocessor clock frequency higher thanthe recommendations of the

manufacturer which allows to execute more instructions at each second. This often requires more power supply at risk of malfunction or evendestruction in case of overheated. Optimization of the executionpath Current microprocessors areoptimized to run more of an instruction per clock cycle, they are microprocessors with parallel threads. In addition they are equipped with procedures that "anticipate"the following instructions withthe help of statistics.

In the race for the power of microprocessors, two methods optimization are incompetition:

RISC technology (Reduced Instruction Set Computer , game simple instructions), quick with simple size instructionsstandardized, easy to manufacture and whose frequency can be of the clock without too muchtechnical difficulties. Technology CISC (complexinstruction set computing), which each complex instruction requires more clock cycles, but who has in his heart manyinstructions prewired. Nevertheless, with the decrease in the size of electronic chips and accelerating clock frequencies, the distinctionbetween RISC and CISC has almost completely disappeared. Wherefamilies trenches existed, today weobserve microprocessors where a RISC internal structure brings power while staying compatible with CISC type use(the Intel x86 family has thus undergone a transition between an organization initiallyvery typical of a CISC structure .Currently she uses a heart RISC very fast, relying on a system of rearrangement of code on the fly) implemented,in part, through memories cache larger and larger, withup to three levels.

Structure **Main articles** : Processor architecture and micro-architecture

.The central unit of a microprocessor essentiallycomprises:

an arithmetic and logical unit(UAL) that performs the

operations; registers that allow the

microprocessor to store

temporarily data; a control unit that controls theentire microprocessor according to the instructions ofthe program.

Some registries have a veryspecial role: flags register,   this register gives the status of the microprocessor at any time, itcan only be read; the program counter (PC, Program Counter), it contains the address of the next

instruction to execute; the stack pointer (SP, Stack Pointer) is the pointer of an areaspecial memory called stack where the arguments arearranged of subroutines and returnaddresses. Only the Program Counter isessential, there are (rare) processors that do not have astatus register or no pointer stack (for example theNS32000).

The control unit can also breakdown: the instruction register, memorizes the code of the instruction to execute; the decoder decodes thisinstruction; the sequencer executes theinstruction, it is he who commands all the organs of themicroprocessor.

Manufacturing Main article : Semiconductordevice fabrication .

The manufacture of a microprocessor is essentiallyidentical tothat of any integrated circuit . It follows a process complex. But the huge size andcomplexity of most microprocessors tends tofurther increase the cost of the operation. The Moore'sLaw , which states that the number of microprocessor transistors ondual silicon chips every 2 years, also indicatesthat production costs double with the degree ofintegration. The manufacture of microprocessors is nowconsidered as one of two factors forincreasing the capacity of manufacturing units (with the constraints related to the manufacture of high capacity memory). Thefinesse of industrial engravinghas reaches 45 nm in 2006[8]. By further reducing the engraving sharpness, the founders come up against the rules of quantum mechanics . Warm up problem

Despite the use of increasinglyfine

engraving techniques,

the heating of the microprocessors remainsapproximately proportional to the square of their given architecture voltage. With voltage, frequency, and acoefficient of fit, one can calculate the dissipated power: This problem is related to another one, that of heat dissipation and so often fans , sources of noise. The Liquid cooling can be used. The use of a paste thermal ensures better conduction of the heat of the processor to the radiator. If the warm-up does not pose a problem major problem for desktoptype applications it in laying for all portable applications. He is technicallyeasy to power and cool a desktop computer. For the portable applications, these are two tricky issues. The mobile phone, laptop, camera the PDA, the MP3 player have abattery that is to ensure that the portable device has a better autonomy. Computer Peripheral A computing device is a device connected to a computer system (computer orgame console$_1$) which adds to the latter features.Device types Devices can generally be classified into two types: input devices and outputdevices. The Input devices are used toprovide information (ordata) to the computer system:keyboard (typing), mouse (pointing), scanner (scanning of paper documents), microphone , webcam, etc. Output devicesare used to bring out Computer system information:screen, printer, built-in speaker, etc. We can also meet peripherals input-output devices that operate in both directions: a **CD-**

player ROM or a **USB** stick, for example, can store data (output). Another category can be added to this one type, these are multifunctiondevices (MFD for Multi F functional Device in English)as a camcorder that works camera, webcam, and externaldisk, or printer that also acts as ascanner. Connecting to the computer On microcomputers, all devicesare connected to the Motherboard by a connectorthat we insert:

either in a port directly soldered to the motherboard; either in an available port onan expansion card , itself plugged into the motherboard.

The expansion card beingremovable, it is easy to replace in case of breakdown or evolution technology.

The operating system installedon the

computer system must have a driver for the device (driver), that is to say a

software responsible for communicating with him and integrating his features to the operatingsystem.

Most devices are removable,that is, they can be disconnected from the central unit without preventing it to work (sometimes you have to turn off the computer beforeremoving the ring road). Internet connection peripherals Input DevicesInput devices

2.1 THE ERA OF MULTIMEDIA AND DIGITAL

With the microcomputer, computers are
become extremely powerful and cheap. They are able to do everything or almost everything: they calculate, draw, and even play music. The invention of the compactdisc (CD) in 1979 by the

anise Philips and Sonywill allow to store a large amount of information (about **600 MB**) on a disc 12 cm in diameter and 1mm thick (**CD-ROM**). The DVD (DigitalVersatile Disc) ,marketed in 1997, can storeeven more data (about 7 times more thanon a CD-ROM). Today, IT has entered thevirtual world all electronic devices, includingin a simple washing machine. It has become indispensable in our everyday life. Internet is a computer networkthat connects computers from all over theworld and who allows to exchange information. The data is

transmitted via telephonelines, cables or satellites. To communicate with eachother, connected computers Internet use a common language (named protocol) and are equippedwith software (or programs) allowing theexchange of data.

2.2 HOW IS INTERNET BORN?

Internet comes from the Arpanet network , which wasdesigned in 1969 by the Agency forResearch Projects Advanced (ARPA, Advanced

Research Project Agency) for the US Department ofDefense. Reserve Originally to the military, theArpanet network gradually extended to universities and

US administrations. In 1990, Arpanet is connectedto many other networks, all based on thesame protocol of communication (**TCP / IP**) : it'sthe birth Internet contraction of "International

Network ", which means" international network "in French. At the beginning of the xxi$_e$ century, the Internet connectsmillions of people around the world. Internet does not belong to nobody and nobody controls it. The users Internet users (known as Internet users) have access to many services, including theWorld Wide Web and the email .

2.2.3 WHAT IS WORLD WIDE WEB?

The term "World Wide Web"(often abbreviated as WWW or Web) means "globalspider web" in French. It's a huge set of pagesso-called Web pages , linkedtogether by of hyperlinks . Just click on alink to be directed to a new page. The information from these pagesmay appear under form of text, images, sound orvideo. Each page belongs to a website ,which is a set of pages created by an individual,a company or an organization. To access web pages, we use abrowser (or browser in English). Browser is a software that allows you toconsult search engines . These enginesare very useful to find information because it exists today several hundred million webpages. In typing one or more keywords ,we get a list pages containing theinformation sought. The Web is not just aboutfinding information. It allows amongother things to recover (or download) electronic files, tobuy or to sell objects. By the way, thegame lovers video can, through theInternet, cope with many other players around the world

2.2.4 HOW CAN WE SUBMIT MESSAGES ON THE INTERNET?

The e-mail makes it possible tosend an email message (also called e-mail) to one or several Internet users. For that, it is enough to know the e-mail address (or e-mailaddress) of the who is sending the messageand being equipped with software messaging . This softwareallows you to type text and to attach a file to his message. If it is connected to Internet, the correspondentreceives the message after a few seconds or minutes(depending on the flow connection lines). The use ofmail electronics can sometimes berisky. In Indeed, many computerviruses are transmit by e-mail and can damage the data stored on the computer. To communicate, users canalso end up in chat rooms (also called "cat" – to pronounce"chat"). These salons allow two or more people to exchange messages in real time. It suffices for that to connect to a website or installsoftware on

his computer.

3.3.1 HOW TO TRANSPORT A CODED INFORMATION IN THE FORM OF ELECTRIC POWER ?

At the beginning of the XIX$_{th}$ century, the work of physicists André-Marie Ampère and Michael Faraday in the field of electromagnetism show the three following elements:

- an electric current can create a field magnetic;
- a magnetic field can create a current electric;
- modify a magnetic field also modifies the electric field associated with it.

However, it is relatively easy to modify a field magnetic: just move the magnet that creates it. In theory therefore, the properties of electromagnetism show that it is possible to carry a signal in the form of an electric current along a conductive thread . To code the signal, just modify the magnetic field in a certain way. At the other end of the wire,the magnetic field will be changed exactly the same way to get thesignal original.

3.3.2 From the bell to the telegram

The electric doorbell is one ofthe applications practices of this discovery. When you press the bell button, closing anelectrical circuit composed inter alia of a coil ofcoiled wire:

creates a magnetic field, which attracts a small hammer to a bell, producing asound. Same time, the movement of the hammer opens the circuit: the magnetic field stops, and thehammer comes back into square. If the doorbell buttonis still pressed, all over again, and the sound continues. The **American Samuel Morse** imagines to lengthen the circuit electric and use the impulses given to the bell like a code: in 1837 is bornthe telegraph, as well as the alphabet that allows for transmit coded messages, theMorse alphabet .The invention is quicklyadopted and unfolds in the whole world, often in thefootsteps of the network of railway ; the telegraph crosseseven the Atlantic in 1866. All thatremains is to improve the device in order to make it ableto carry the human voice.

3.3.3 THE "FATHERS" OF THE TELEPHONE

The invention of the telephone is generally attributed to the American

Alexander Bell in1876 but the reality is a little more complex thanthat.

It is certain that it's Bell who filed the first realpatent about the phone, and he's thefirst to know successfully market itsinvention. Among the most unfortunatecompetitors in the race to patent but whose ideas

haveinfluenced Bell and who have so contributed to the inventionof the phone, one can to quote :

- the Frenchman CharlesBourseul , employee of telegraph, which publishes anarticle describing the principle telephone in 1854;
- the engineer Antonio Meucci ,Italian immigrant to the
    United States, which installs a device capable of   transmit the voices betweenthe different pieces of his

house in 1855; lack of financial means, it does not fails to commercialize hisinvention, nor to file a patent;

- the German Johann Reiss ,who builds a camera able to transmit music over along
distance in 1861;

- the Italian Innocenzo Manzetti , who makes public in 1865 an apparatus similar tothat of Johann Reiss,
sort of musical telegraphtransmitting very badly the human voice;

  - the American Elisha Gray ,who reaches about
  - same point as Bell, but files itspatent a few
  - hours after him ...;
  - - finally, the American Alexander Bell who, in 1876,
  - files the patent for the telephone and then founds thefirst
  - company dedicated to itsmarketing,

the Bell
- Telephone Company (which will become the powerful
- telecommunications company AT & T).

3.3.4 THE PRINCIPLE AND COMPONENTS OF PHONE

- Current phones are based onthe same principle
- than that of Bell: they transform the sound wave of
- the voice into an electriccurrent whose
- characteristics are similar tothose of the wave
- sound, then retransform at theother end of the
- circuit the electric current intosound vibrations .
- The microphone and thespeaker, to talk and hear
- When talking in the microphone imagined by Bell,
- a membrane vibrates: thiscauses the oscillation of a
- magnet and therefore the modification of his field
- magnetic. The magnet produces an

electric current
- in the coil of conductive wirelocated nearby; the
- characteristics of this electriccurrent are similar
- to those of sound produced. Atthe other end of the line, a
- similar device (but inverse),the speaker ,
- reproduces the sound wave.
- Bell's microphone is veryinsensitive. It is necessary
- wait for the work of ThomasEdison (the inventor of
- phonograph), by Emil Berliner(the inventor of the disc),
- and especially the adoption ofthe coal microphone (put
- at the 1877 point by the American David Edward Hughes)
- so that the voice really becomes audible to the other
- end of the line.
- Current microphones are quite different from
- first microphones. They aremore

reliable,
- more powerful and less bulky.
- They rest

- yet on the same electromagnetic principle.
- The common thread carriesthe information
- Between the microphone of the transmitter and the receiveris
- unwind the wire or telephonecable .
- The first cables used are thoseof the
- telegraph : most major cities in America
- Northern and Western Europe, already connected to the
- telegraph, adopt the telephone before the end of the
- XIX
- th century, and subscriptionsare increasing.
- However, the telegraphnetwork is inadequate for
- deployment of the telephone,since the links established
- are fixed, connecting two postsin the

- manner of a interphone: it is finally abandoned while a
- dedicated network is set up.
- The first cables
- are made of iron or bronze, then of copper.
- The first communications have a scope enough
- low, the voice weakening rapidly as
- the signal travels along the wire. The relay, expensive and
- moderately effective, are first installed. They
- are replaced in 1906 by the first
- amplifiers (the triode of the American Lee of
- Forest): the extension of the network no longer seems to have Limits
- Quickly, the phone is a victim of its success and
- a rather narrow starting infrastructure. The
- multiplication of lines requires to install

- " Standards ", where operators (mainly
- operators) are working toconnect the wires
- to connect subscribers to eachother. Progress in
- this area allow the rapid development of
- automatic switches - operatorswill still have good days in
- front of them:
- in France for example, the automation of the network
- only completed in the 1970s!
- But the biggest challenge is thecable itself:
- how to carry an everincreasing number of
- phone calls? How to equip large cities where live several
- millions of
- people? The first phones aremore
- effect of the phone booth asthe phone
- staff - especially since we oftenhave to wait

- the line is released, either up to standard or after
- this one ... Engineers arecontent to first
- twist several thousand threads, before inventing a
- system in 1918 (modulation of currents
- carriers) which allows to carry several
- conversations at the same timeon the same line; this
- system is further improved inthe 1930s by

the development of a special structure (structure

 concentric or coaxial) whichmakes it possible to   transmit several thousand conversations simultaneously. Today, the telephone networkcontinues to expand. Where the cable network is insufficient (between continents or in the mostisolated places), the phone can also use thesatellites of telecommunications or evensome radio waves . For twenty years, the telephone network also serves to connect to theglobal network Internet .The dial or keypad dials the number The first phones did not have adial or keyboard: pick up his phonecould reach an operator, who manuallylinked the two interlocutors. Then theautomation of connections gave birth to thenumber of phone , which identifies each subscriber so

unique. In France, currently, the first figure   (after"0")

means the area where thesubscriber lives; he is   followed of 8 digits. When we callFrance since abroad, the area code must be preceded by the international dialing code of France, which is the 33rd. When we call from France to abroad, must first dial the "00", then the code the called country, and then the area code if necessary, and finally the number of his correspondent. Older phones are equipped with a mobile circular dial . Current phones are rather have a keyboard that produces either pulses (the number of pulses represents the composite number), i.e. tones (each digit corresponds to a note).

4 ENSURING THE THREAD

The wireless born in the 1950s, when we began to ship

conversations between different points of the networkby the wave path, using the wirelessnetwork terrestrial or telecommunications satellites . This technology (and especially the miniaturization of electromagnetic wavetransceivers) gives birth to the mobile phone, which allows call and be joined all over theworld. The mobile phone with only onetransmitter relatively weak, it needs towork to be pretty close to a relay . Tocover a territory given, it is necessary to installa large number of relay The evolution of telecommunication technologies seems to be moving towards a certain convergence:

the phones of the house havealready freed themselves

wire (they are "wireless"around their

base; should quickly join the phones' from the street ", mobiles). So, both inside and outside, we would phone withone small device, more and more personal, freeof any wire or any based. Meanwhile, current phonesknow how to do well more than just carrying thevoice; more and more, they already integrate or willintegrate new services: e-mail, GPS navigation system,sending and receiving images, photos, data, radio broadcasts or television, etc.

Context :

Many technological projects initiatedby aid agencies

Bilateral and multilateral development took place during the last

decade (2000-2010), in Mali. Afterthe World Summit on Society

information in Geneva in December2003, Swiss Cooperation has

decided to install communitymultimedia centers in three African countries (Mali, Mozambique,Senegal) in partnership with UNESCO. These Community Multimedia Centers (CMCs) were installed in several rural communes of Mali andgave birth to a new generation of users (users). USAID also

installed CLICs (Local Informationand Communication Center) in

rural and urban communes to enablethe population

disadvantaged to have access toinformation technology and

communication. Social networks (Face book, Badoo, twiter etc.) have also

attracted new users to TV centers inrural areas and in cybercafés in urban communes and inthe capital (Bamako). For some users thesetechnologies have always existed (these have the Digital Natives) anddo not necessarily know the evolution of technological tools,that is to say classical media ICT.

The concerns of the technical andfinancial partners (PTF) which is build the capacity of each other toreduce the divide digital between north and south orinside a country has created a new digital divide between generations (young and old people) and between geographicalareas (urban municipalities and rural). This gap has also widenedbetween those who have the financial resources to accesstechnological tools and those who do not have one.

4.4.2 OBJECT OF THE CONTRIBUTION

Our contribution aims to bring newexpertise to the field of information and communication technologies in the fieldof

Mali and more precisely on their appropriation by the local populations. It is also a question of how thisappropriation by different communities fits into arelevant approach for the development of communicationtechnologies in Mali. Mastery

impacts of ICT projects on different communities we will make it possible to control the technological settlements for the future research. The emergence of new users allows the opening up and opening up to otherterritories. This research made it possible to understand thatthe reflections of the different users depend on their social environment. These new users are generally

influenced by those whotrain them to the tools technological or by their politicalparty. Our research allowed us to understand the new areas ofproduction and reception of messages by new users ofcommunication technologies in Mali. This work also allowed us tounderstand the behaviors and reflections of thisaudience.

4.4.3 THEORETICALFRAMEWORK

In this article, we present the theoretical framework that allowed us to elaborate our research. Our theoreticalframework first describes the approaches developed by experts and specialists in other fields such as geography (Cheneau-Loquay, 2000; Eveno, 1997), economics

(Gabas, 2004) and sociology (Blanchard,2004) who are interested inissues and uses information and communication technologies.

4.4.4 INTRODUCTION

The problem of development through ICT continues

to fuel controversies. Despite the current context marked

through the intensive use of information in many activities, the contribution of ICTs to Africa's development remains still disputed.

In relation to thiscontinent, these tools are considered by their detractorsto be an unproductive luxury classic development priorities.

While recognizing the relevance of these arguments,this

However, the study aims toidentify weaknesses and to demonstrate through theoretical reasoningand practical examples, that ICTs are now a decisive factorin the development of Africa, or even a prerequisite to the realization of it.

The study also builds on the rich literature problematic of ICT for development. Quite frequently, news aboutAfrica is marked by acts of calamity (famine, diseases, coups d'état bloody, civil wars, natural disasters, etc.). In such a context of permanent misery, it is not at all surprising that thedevelopment planners and at the same time, sensitive andpriority issues such as health, food, drinking water, education, electrification or the roads? Faced with suchchallenges, he appears almost legitimate for many Africans todevelop a negative vision, even hostile, vis-à-vis these ICTs that they actually learn to discover. Also, rather than considering them as a real opportunity for

development, do they consider them useless, even intrinsically unfit for development and therefore not

deserving States should make substantialinvestments and this, despite flattering speeches aimed at believing in amembership to societal project on ICT (see quote policy makers African countries, in the prioritization of their development projects, attach little importance to information technology and communication they consider,after all, as needs really secondary, even superfluous, according to anAfrican president. Paradoxically, despite the existence in most countries a ministry specifically dedicated to this sector, which issupposed to be the promotion because supposedly important. How, indeed, have the real willto initiate projects and mobilize resources for infrastructure development still perceived as an unproductive luxury while previous).

These reluctance towards ICT,which we honestly can not

challenge the relevance (giventhe aforementioned adverse context), However, this reflects less the rejection of ICT than the difficulty of planners and decision-makersto establish an operational link between these and development [Ossama, 2001]. However, the relevance of this position does not exhaust the complexity of the debate. This is not because we ignore the usefulness of something that thisone

has no value in reality. Pretend, simply on the basis of

prejudices or from ignorance,that such a sector is a priority and that another is secondary is aManichean vision and

reductive which can lead toerrors with serious consequences for a continent where the development process is down In all areas. In addition,compare or contrast needs or necessities of different natures (food, water, clinics, roads, etc. versus ICT)is an ineffective approach in practice, for the simple reason that these needs haveroles different, but rather complementary. About preciselyfrom the classic "Africa's priorities"argument for

 disqualify ICT as a factor of development in Africa, it should be emphasized that this is an argument that can be acarrier of risks. If at best, byprioritizing, such a stereotype is not intended to legitimize the idea that

information and communication technologieswould be really a luxury for this continent, at worst we can fearthat it diverts some African investorsand planners aware of modern developmentstrategies, these tools now indispensable. Africa,which missed the era of

Industrial Revolution (with the

disastrous consequences that this has spawned on its development), can it afford to miss that of the InformationRevolution, under the pretext that it would have other priorities to satisfy first? In truth, on this question, thereis a problem of lighting and information on how information technology and communication cancontribute, in a way significant, to the economicand social development of populations and territories inAfrica While it is undeniable that thelack of roads, for example, in a region is a major development problem, it is equally indisputable that insociety and the economy of information where we livenow, the new factors of

productivity, attractivenessand competitiveness are the ability to access information and exploitit as needed.

Considering, moreover, thatICT investments can not

oppose those to consent in theso-called priority areas,

rather, we think that in manycases ICTs are today essential to carry outcertain projects considered

priority. Following this logic, the Maitland Report [ITU, 1985]criticizes the perception that telecommunications would beless vital and less achievements such as foodproduction, adduction of water or electrification, forexample. He says strongly, contrary, that telecommunications constitutean element essential part of the development process, which is complementary other achievements. In this sense, he considers that they are tools that can increase the productivity and efficiency of agriculture, industry, commerce, etc. Where from the importance of having ICT infrastructures that allow to access information easilyand to exploit it will.

5 THE CONCEPT

1The concept "ICTs fordevelopment" refers to the use of ICTs for development purposes socioeconomic. In this perspective, it aims to encourage

the integration of these tools inthe different human activities, whether it is the introductionof informatics into the enterprises, in the education,health or

these are major innovative development projects such as e-government, digitaldevelopment of the territory, etc. Due to the growing importance taken byinformation in all types of activities, ICTs assert now, in developed and emerging countries, as toolshelping to formalize development strategies (to nationally and locally). Indeed, information, of which ICT is the vector, has become a strategic resource. In this context, what is true for developed and emerging countries the same for countries poor and especially for Africa?

The "ICT at the service of the development " is it, in relation to Africa, a simple slogan (in the light of the classic development priorities of this continent) or does it reflect a reality? 1 We have instead favored a broad view of the subject (at the African).2To answer these questions, we structured the study in two main parts: the firstconsists of an approach the theoretical issue of development through ICT. Forthis to do, it is inspired in part by the literature on the subject. The theoretical reasoning is neverenough to convince, the Part Two consists of practicalexamples (supported by statistical data) drawn inparticular from the Ivoriancontext. This is so a study that combinestheoretical approach and approach empirical.5.5.1 THEORETICALAPPROACH TO PROBLEM OF 5.5.2 DEVELOPMENT BY

ICT 3In spite of field observation (facts) and testimonials

which tend to show that ICTsare

increasingly being used, not more like simple media ofcommunication or tools of facilitation of work, but as realfactors of development and promotion ofa territory, the debate on their inopportune nature in Africa (unproductive luxury for a continent still plagued by many miseries)still remains relevant [Gado, 2008; Robert A.-C., 2000, etc.]. Hence the need for conduct this theoretical reflection to try to clarify theissue.

5.5.3 TENACIOUS OBSTACLES THAT OPPOSE A ADMISSION OF ICT AS FACTORS DEVELOPMENT IN AFRICA

4Two obstacles are traditionally opposed to theadmission of ICT as development factors inAfrica. In the first place, the continent's urgency argument that the priority be given to conventional needs (food, water

drinking, public health, education, roads, etc.) [AnneCécile Robert, 2000]. Secondly, the particular difficulty of measuringthe economic and socialimportance of ICT in development.

5.5.4 THE ARGUMENT OF LUXURY IMPRODUCTIVE THAT CONSTITUTE ICT INRELATION TO NUMEROUS PRIORITIES FORDEVELOPMENT IN AFRICA

5As often, news about Africa is marked by acts of calamity (famine, diseases, coups d'etatbloody, civil wars, natural disasters, etc.). In such a context of permanent misery, it is not at all surprising that the

development planners andpolicy makers African   countries, in the prioritization of their development projects, attach little importance to information technology and communication they consider,after all, as needs really secondary, even superfluous, according to anAfrican president cited by Jacques Bonjawo [2011, p.17]. And this, paradoxically, in despite the existence in most countries of a ministry specially dedicated to this sector, supposed to promote itbecause that supposed important. 6How, indeed, have the real will to initiate projects and to mobilize resources forinfrastructure development still perceived as an unproductive luxury while at the same time, sensitive andpriority issues such as health, food, drinking water,education, electrification

or the roads? Faced with such challenges, he appears almost legitimate for many Africans to develop a negative vision, even hostile, vis-à-vis these ICTs that they actually learn todiscover. Also, rather than considering them as a real opportunity for development, do they consider them useless, even intrinsically unfit for development and therefore not deserving States should make substantialinvestments and this, despite flattering speeches aimed at believing in amembership to a societal project on ICT (see quote previous). 7This reluctance towards ICTs,which we honestly cannot challenge the relevance (giventhe aforementioned adverse context),

However, this reflects less the rejection of ICT than the difficulty of planners and decision-makersto establish an operational link between these and development [Ossama, 2001]. However, the relevance of this position does not exhaust the complexity of the debate. This

is not because we ignore the usefulness of something that thisone has no value in reality. Pretend, simply on the basis of prejudices or from ignorance, that such a sector is a priorityand that another is secondary is aManichean vision and reductive which can lead toerrors with serious consequences for a continent where the development process is down In all areas. In addition,compare or contrast needs or necessities of different natures (food, water, clinics, roads, etc. versus ICT)is an ineffective approach in practice, for the simple reason that these needs haveroles different, but rather complementary. About preciselyfrom the classic "Africa's priorities"argument for disqualify ICT as a factor ofdevelopment in Africa, it should be emphasized that this is an argument that can be acarrier of risks. If at best, byprioritizing, such a stereotype is not intended to legitimize the idea that information and communication technologies would be really a luxury for this continent, at worst we can fearthat it diverts some African investorsand planners aware of modern developmentstrategies, these tools now indispensable. Africa,which missed the era of Industrial Revolution (with thedisastrous consequences that this has spawned on its development), can it afford to miss that of the Information Revolution, under the pretext that it would have otherpriorities to satisfy first? 8In truth, on this question, there is a problem of lighting and information on how information technology and communication can contribute, in a way significant, to the economicand social development of populations and territories inAfrica. 9If it is indisputable that thelack of roads, for example, in a region is a major development problem, it is equally indisputable that insociety and the economy of information where we livenow, the new factors of productivity, attractivenessand competitiveness are the ability to access information and exploitit as needed.

Considering, moreover, thatICT investments can not oppose those to consent in theso-called priority areas, rather, we think that in many cases ICTs are today essential to carry outcertain projects considered

priority. Following this logic, the Maitland Report [ITU, 1985]criticizes the perception that telecommunications would beless vital and less

achievements such as food production, adduction

of water or electrification, for example. He says strongly,

contrary, that telecommunications constitutean element essential part of the development process, which is complementary other achievements. In this sense, he considers that they are

tools that can increase the productivity and efficiency of agriculture, industry, commerce, etc. Where from the importance of having ICTinfrastructures that allow to access information easilyand to exploit it will. 10It is only once that certaintyabout the importance of

ICT has been established that itwill become relatively easier for governments, planners andinvestors to consider serious initiatives to mobilizethe necessary resources to integrate them harmoniously in the projects of development. ICTs are not aproblem totally decoupled from other development problems. They arerather interacting with them. 11The second obstacle to the admission of ICTs as instruments in the service of development in Africa lies in thedifficulty even in measuring the economic and social weightof these tools in development.

5.5.5 THE SPECIAL DIFFICULTY TO MEASURE THE ECONOMIC AND SOCIAL WEIGHT OF ICT IN DEVELOPMENT. A REALOBSTACLE BUT Surmountable

Concretely, it is difficult toperceive the role of ICTs

 in development while we are measuring statistically the developmentimplications of sectors like agriculture, health, even scientific research. In each one

of these sectors, we can seethem through the increase in agricultural yields resulting from the use of inputs, improving lifeexpectancy, the results operational in different industrial areas as well as in States' economic developmentand defense strategies. The perception of the role ofICT is complicated by the difficulty even to measure the economic weight of the sector. Also, manifestation of ICTs at the macroeconomic level appears for many economists assomething of nature paradoxical (see below). This feeling of paradox stems probably reflections of Robert Merton Solow, who was watchingin 1987 that the computer age was visible everywhere except in

statistics on productivity (" Wesee the computer age everywhere except in the productivity statistics ") . Thisantinomy was quickly dubbed the "paradox of productivity" or " Solow's paradox " , which reflects the fact that the growthof computing would not have led, contrary to hopes maintained, a revival of growthduring the period 1970-1990. 4 The Berkeley Round Table onInternational Economy is considered as one of the leading multimedia centers

However, according to other economic analysts, this paradoxdoes not would not really be one. Among these, we can mentionStephen Cohen and John Zysman [2001,pp. 34-35], two teachers of the American University of Berkeley in California, which by co-chaired the Berkeley RoundTable on International Economy. For these two researchers, the consequence of

the introduction of computersis crucial, particularly their implications in the formsof business organization.

They specify, however, that it is less the number of computers than the global change that these induce in the functioning of the economythat increases productivity across a number of parameters: geographical mobility of thelabor force, flexibility in relation to type of employment, creation companies, shifting investments from novelty to another, evolution oforganizations. This transformation general organizational structure would in turn generate productivity that we would seequite clearly in the sectors and countries where computerization and ICT are very widespread in activities. 14Student for its part the effects of the added value of themarkets Rainer Kuhlen [1997, p.177], aspecialist in information, notes that "at the macroeconomic level, the development of an information sector generates structural changes in the entireeconomy. This development affects the gross national product and the employmentsituation, and gives hope for generaleconomic growth . 15Cohen and Zysman (citedabove) point to another fact significant: the greater the useof ICT in activities and their effect is easily felt because, they explain, a high rate of ICT penetrationnecessarily entails a cost reduction in other sectorsof the economy (including services). 16If the statistical difficulty inmeasuring the economic weightand ICT is very real, it remains truethat this hurdle can be overcomenowadays due to a better knowledge of the role of thesetools. In addition, the change of paradigm characterized by the advent of a society and a The information economy isbecoming more and more understanding of the role of ICTs in development.

6. THE CHANGE OF PARADIGM IMPOSES ONE POSITIVE VISION OF THE ROLE OF ICT IN THE DEVELOPMENT

This paradigm shift is reflected in the growing role of information in the workings of society and the economy modern [Toffler, 1991; ITU,1982; Samara, 1999]. 18The information society ischaracterized by the reorganization of society around production, processing, dissemination andintensive consumption of information in virtually

all human activities. This reorganization makes necessarily rely on technologynetworks and services from information and communication. As for theeconomy of information (sometimes referred to as "new economy" or" net economy "), it is defined asa new structure world economy in which theproduction of goods and information services is predominant in the creation of

wealth and jobs. These realities refer

to the concepts of

knowledge society and knowledge economy. These twodynamics concomitant are driven by ICTswhich have accelerated the transition to an intangible society andeconomy. In such a context, the new factors of productivity and competitiveness become creativity, knowledge, intelligence and expertise. One realizes that developmentchallenges related to ICT are real if we know how to look forthem. From then on, a vision more The positive role of ICTs in development can be appreciated different levels:

5 Information is understood here in its broad sense; that is tosay, data (economic, financial. 19a) ICTs make access easier and cheaper to information5 at a time whenmastery

of it has become a key factor in developmentand the ability to access it, manipulating and diffusing it conditions the feasibility and sustainability of socio-economic development.

(20b) ICTs give African countries the opportunity formore great economic, commercial and cultural integration into the world, provided, of course, thatthese countries are fully aware and that they makethe investments necessary to allow them toseize opportunities. 21c) Telematics networks offerincreased productivity and productivity competitiveness through the modification of the management system enterprises. Indeed, modern trade is based on "fast response", "real time", "competition based on time ", etc. African countries (mainly South Africa and the Maghreb countries) manage to meet these criteriathrough the existence of good ICT infrastructures have become more competitive in the globalization of trade. 22d) In terms of spatial planning, the location of businesses and populations in fragile areas (isolation, natural disinheritance, marginalization due toremoteness by report to the capitals) is imperative today through the ability of these areas toprovide a modern and attractive based on the flow ofinformation, organized from efficient telematics networksand services. By influencing the organization and dynamicsof the territories and, as a result, localization of activities andmen, ICTs have become a social necessity, an economicasset and a political and strategic focus. 23rd) An e-government wouldallow our States to be more effective and better servecitizens through: faster circulation of information in digital form, communication and sharing of information between central directorates anddecentralized services, dematerialization of certain administrative procedures (tele-procedures via dedicated networks or via the Internet). 24The contemporary societyand economy are now strong information content. It has become, if not the first product,at the very least one of the main consumer products common. The informationconsumption of individuals, businesses, administrations,communities and organizations is growing at an accelerated pace. Certainly, it does not exist standard to scientifically evaluate this consumption as it is done for electricity or forwater; but, obviously, this consumption increasesexponentially and translates eloquently in the increase inmonthly expenses of telecommunication. This has led to a new economic model and in which ICTs are unavoidable.25If we consider the current paradigm shift determinedby the weight of the information and its vector, andwhich escapes obviously not Africa, the question is not so much to know whether or not ICTs are able to effectively help development of poor countries. The fundamental question is rather to know how to best use them for the development of these countries. The importance ofICTs for countries the poor, however, is not to besought in their ability to directly to provide economicand social progress to all layers of the population. Such avision blurs the understanding and support the pessimistic theses, as the

economies and poor societiesare still too little digitized so that the direct effects of ICTare quite perceptible.

6.6.1 ICT IS ACTUALLYINSTRUMENTS AT THE SERVICE OF DEVELOPMENT IN AFRICA

For at least two reasons, it canbe said that ICTs constitute tools for development in Africa

6.6.2 LIMITATIONS OF THE ACCOUNTING APPROACH

6 Regarding the informal economy of the telephony sector

mobile phone, an article from 27Two indicators are generally used by economists networks to try to properlyappreciate the weight of ICTs in development: there is, on the one hand, the share of the sectors of activity related to thehandling or processing of information in the constitution of **GNP** and,on the other hand, the number ofjobs these areas of activity. These two indicators are referred to asterms of diffusing factors or direct factors because they aredirectly appreciable effects. The diffusing factor or factor The direct effect of ICT is the direct creation of progress economic and employment opportunities through theactivities of equipment, service and manufacture (when it exists). We can talk in this case of output , that is to say yield. Only under this report, the vast ICT sector[network and telephone services, internetservice providers, data carriers, resellers of services, public broadcasters and deprived of audiovisual programs, intermediate jobs orappendices (IT specialists, convenience stores, equipment distributors and telecommunications, etc.)represents currently an important link inAfrican economies. In a particularly gloomy economic context on thecontinent, the global telecommunicationssector is currently one of those

which generate the most foreign investments, jobs andtherefore of wealth creation in Africa. An investigation by Ernst & Young reveals, for example,that in 2008 ICTs accounted for6% of Ivory Coast's GDP with aturnover of around 700 billion FCFA (1.06 billion euros). For the same year In 2008, direct investment inthe sector amounted to 120 billion FCFA (0.182 billioneuros), and over the period from 1997 to 2008 investments amounted to 820billion FCFA (1.25 billion euros). According to that study, no othersector could not achieve such remarkable results. He It should also be noted that thetrend in other African countries is broadly similar to that observedin Ivory Coast (see the same study). Moreover, a report fromHot Telecom (another consultingfirm), quoted by pan-African magazine Telecom Network (April 2011), notes that the share of theICT sector in the GDP of South Africa,Tunisia and Tanzania, 2009, was 7%, 10% and 20%respectively. Which shows that the sector is dynamic everywhere.

To this must beadded a sector informal, particularly flourishing and dynamic(especially in the field of mobile cellulartelephony), which was able to generate hundreds of thousands (evenmillions) of small jobs and substantial income for peopleof all ages and genders who exercise it wherever thenetworks are available. 28However, for a long time,some economists have gloated over the fact that these indicators were insignificant in the constitution **GNP** of developed countries. Moreover, in poor countries, difficulty remained, in the absence of reliable statistics concerning sector and data on the share ofthe informal economy telecommunications, to reallyevaluate the economic weight of **TIC**. In addition, the strictly accounting approach (in and the number of jobs),although it generally to understand the economicand social weight of the ICT sector, However, it is not sufficient, even relevant, to capture the role true of these tools in the wholeof mechanics socioeconomic. That is to say,it is not very operative for appreciate the full and real contribution of ICT to the process global development. Therefore,it is essential to distinguish ICT production(diffusing factors or factors their use in economic activitiesand (ie their structuring factors orfactors indirect). This approach seemsto us more effective because, exceeding the often incomplete frame ofthe figures (search for the contribution

GNP and growth, the numberof jobs generated), integrates the parameters of empirical observation, that is, the finding, the facts that economicarithmetic does not reach

always to seize. It's probably tohave neglected this

dimension of the analysis thatled Robert Solow to talk about paradox of productivity thatmany economic analysts

reject more and more now. In recent years, the accountingapproach has shown its because there is evidence today that shows that ICTs are instruments inthe service of

development (see concreteexamples below).

6.6.2 THE STRUCTURING ORFACTOR FACTOR INDIRECT: A MORE OPERATIVE INDICATOR ASSESSING THE ROLE OF ICT IN THE DEVELOPMENT

30The structuring or indirectfactor of ICT (which has existed since long time, but is ignored or even contested in some cases) stimulates the dynamism of other sectors of activity by facilitating the execution of multiple tasks in companies or in the administration. It is also about improving comfort social and security of populations through, for example, the phone and the internet that weuse to communicate in many circumstances. Television and radio have become essential elements of our daily lives and no one can to deprive too long in town or in the country. We can speak here of input because in such cases, rather ICTs act as a socio-economic input. It is difficult to appreciate the extent and the real scope. However, a pragmatic way to evaluate this dimension of ICT in development simply consists of imagine the consequence of their more or less prolonged deprivation in the circumstances and the multiple activities where we have the need and the habit of making use of it. One thing is certain, this factor, albeit indirect, affects the rationalization and management of

different activities (companies, administrative services,

government development programs) as well as on our everyday way of life. These factors in turn influence the gross national product, onour performance and therefore on the development. The work ofresearcher J. Feather (1994),cited by F. Ossama [2001, p.66], for example, show that the use of ICT, by modifying the management system of companies and institutions, leads to significant structural changes in economic activities. Thus, theinformation would significantly influence on the production and distribution of goods, wouldserve as a support services such as transportation, banks, insurance,and give an additional basis ofcompetitiveness. 31As a reflection, for companies, administrations, communities, developmentagencies and individuals, the question should not be so much that of the direct role of the technology itself, but ratherthat of the consequences organizational aspects of theirrespective activities, on the lifestyle of individuals. It's the understanding of this

causality, it seems to us, whichwould make it possible to better various development issuesrelated to ICT.

32The structuring factor of ICTs on the economy of Africancountries For the moment, it is rather marginal because of the fact that in these countries are stillscarcely digitized, and should make efforts on thisside. Which means, progressively, the telematization must touch the different fields of activity: industries, services, administrations public authorities, localcommunities and even agriculture. It's a requirement of our time. Whatshould have the effect of to make these activities moredynamic and above all more competitive.

33 The following examples show the concrete implication of ICTs in the development of African countries:

34- At the spatial planning level: 7 Comsat (Communication Satellite Corporation) is the name of

the American company in charge of communication.

35 The observation shows that the regions traditionally

characterized by a notorious insufficiency in development of all types aretherefore particularly

feared and marginalized officials and operators

which consider them as territories inhospitable. To open up and boost these regions, now uses ICT. The State of Côted'Ivoire, for example, has 1993, in part, to telecommunications, through a satellite transmission project called Comsat, judiciously integrated into anexpanded program including a project road. In order to ensure full coverage of the Ivorian territory radio and television reception,the government of Ivory Coast

signed in 1993 a contract withthe American company Comsat for the routing of nationalprogram signals. In

1996, the project entered its operational phase and made it possible to serve the country in excellent listening and video conditions. By connecting disadvantaged regions to the rest of the country and to world, these combined projects have brought significant changes in local development, changes taking place translated in particular in terms of breaking the marginalization geographic and regional attractiveness in economic termsand

administrative. Unfortunately,the 2002 civil war provoked the destruction of many relaystations receiving

signals, plunging wholeregions back into initial situation of marginality. The post-election crisis of November 2010 to April 2011 further aggravated this situation.The look at the importance of thisequipment in terms planning and information issues, their rehabilitation is essential. 36- At the level of modern management of agricultural activities: 8 Using the GP features combined with the system Geographic Information (GIS). 37Agriculture and the peasantry are the traditionalpillar of most African economies. But, paradoxically enough,it is the sector that has benefited the least from telecommunications. Yet the analysis shows that this sector has a lot to gain from using these instruments. That's what in recent years, many cooperatives Ivorian farmers who are nowusing ICT to manage more dynamically their activities. During a field survey company in 2003 as part of thedrafting of our thesis doctorate [Loukou, 2005], wehave indeed observed that in the campaigns, that the phone,the fax and more and more the Internet are now useful tools to helpmanage more dynamics of agricultural cooperative activities in Côted'Ivoire. This trend has even strengthened over time.Otherwise, the advent of precision farming, which is a technique innovative cultivation, of practical application simple buteffective in terms of increasing quantityand improving quality production and preservation ofthe environment, opens up even wider perspectives of an advantageous use **ICT** in the national agriculturalsector, particularly for many agro-industrialists.38- At the level of the integration of some activitiesintended Regional 9 Established in 1996, theRegional Stock Exchange (BRVM) is a financial institution.

ICTs today play a leading role in fully telematised and decentralized operation of theStock Exchange Securities Commission (BRVM)of eight African countries from West. Without them, thisregional development structure could never have seen the lightof day and serve the interests of the countries up. Beyond the facilitation ofthe routing of the orders of stock market (electronically, inreal time and simultaneously for all stakeholders in each of the 8 countries), ICT offers a beautiful example of modeling new forms and possibilities organization and dynamisationof activities on spaces vast and remote geographical areas. At the same time, they promote necessary economic integration and regional policyfor

countries with weak economies consideredindividually.

40- At the level of interurban monetary transactions:

10 The so-called electronic money

transfer is so successfuleverywhere in Africa that independently

41The advent of ICT has completely changed the way traditional money transfer in Africa, which remains an activityhighly developed because of the financial dependence of many people in rural areas vis-à-vis those urban areas, and sometimes vice versa. Now, the transfer says electronic money is the most common procedure for sending money between two cities in a country. This procedure is considered more reliable and faster, the result isalmost instantaneous. Indeed, in the moments that follow thedeposit of money in an agency approved, and provided that he is informed by mobile phone,the

recipient can immediately withdraw

the money that hasbeen transferred to a local branch ofthe various companies that operate in thisarea. Equipped with a room identity, he has only to communicate the transfernumber, the code secret as well as the amount ofmoney that have previously been communicated over thetelephone by the issuer. 42New electronic moneytransaction systems offer real opportunities to putICT in the service of development. They are another obvious example of modeling of new forms of ICTuse in the service development in Africa, wherethe rate of banking services remains still very weak. Of course, beyond these fewconcrete examples, the multispectral applications ofICT in development socio-economic conditions of African countries extend to other

6.6.3 RECOMMENDATIONS FOR SUCCEEDING IMPLEMENTATION OF A PROJECT

7. CASE STUDIES

7.1 INTRODUCTION

Recent years have seen aresurgence of interest in Empowerment of the poorthrough inexpensive and cost effective information and communications(ICT) affordable. To achieve this, weneed pro-poor policies and regulatory frameworks that create an enabling environment for development of an appropriate and affordable infrastructure in underserved areas, large-scale initiatives that offer easily accessible and affordable services for the poor, sustainable projects with sufficient funds, commitment and project ownership, humanresource allocation sufficient to maintain it, andfinally which gives the poor tools toimprove their conditions and quality of life. This overview summarizes

opportunities offered by new technologies and questions posed by theirimplementation in projects

communities, especially inpoor communities, marginalized and underserved. It is rare that the initiative of asingle institution or ministry

alone achieve equitable access,and it is not the territory of only public entities or large private telecom companies: theefforts to provide to serve unattractive markets (generally poorer regions

and more distant) are mostoften really important for traditional providers oftelecom services, for low financial returns. To reachthe most disadvantaged societies, it is therefore necessary to adopt a pro-poor policy approach, which can be found in the detailed analysis in the Political Questions and of this resource kit.

A wide variety of solutions have nevertheless been proposedfor to meet the needs of underserved populations,including development of innovative business models, which involve participation of various owners and actors like theauthorities

municipal and local governments, cooperatives,ownership models or community leadership, orsector models whether large corporations orsmall businesses

local. As a general rule, these innovative models are implemented on a small scale, they usecheap technologies such as wireless networks and free software, and the community is strongly involved in various ways: it contributes according to the principle of personal laborinput to install the devices or buy shares toprovide the capital of launch. Implement ICT access projectsin communities poor and marginalized peoplepresents many difficulties, including lack of access to ICTinfrastructure, lack of electricity to operate theappliances, the lack of knowledge of available technologies in a growing market continually evolving, lack ofresource skills human resources to develop, install and maintain technologies,lack of access by large-scale projects to sources of funding, lack of public awareness of the benefits access to ICTs, the difficulties in finding their way local bureaucracies, and thelack of openness to **ICT** political and regulatory environments. In addition, it iscommon to deal with gender inequalities in this area, whichrequire specific interventions to redress the situation. Three case studies will here part ofhow some projects These issues and lessons havebeen addressed by

could be useful for otherprojects: The Agrarian Information System of Peru's Huaral Valley The wireless network projectof Nepal The Mozambican Medical Information Network (MHIN).

This overview looks at implementation from the perspectives following:

A brief overview of the different technologies availableand the how they were used. Examplesinclude a

wide variety of sectors and applications to illustrate how poor communities havebenefited from these technologies. New business models and theirimplementation in communities. Recommendations to successfully implement projects.

7.7.2 CHOICE OF INNOVATIVE TECHNOLOGIES

ICTs refer to a variety of ancient technologies, new and emerging markets, including radio, television,

voice and data transmission via fixed line, telephony over internet protocol (VoIP), and more recently the development of new technologies in mobile telephony and the many wireless technologies. The recent development of ICTs and opportunities they offer, such as the internet and technology mobile, threaten the mainstream main stream media and reduce consumption, so that they are turning more and more more towards mobile and online applications to attract their audience and allow them tocontribute content - thus increasing the possibilities of interactivityfor citizens. The choice of technology canbe decisive for measurement in which ICTs are useful to thepoor. The most technology accessible remains generally radio, and the growing number ofcommunity radios play a vital role in providing information adapted locally topoor communities. Since 1990, it has been made great case for the offer of access telephone and internet to communities underserved by public internet access points. Many countries have created auniversal service and access funds by following public authorities to providethe necessary funds for the implementation of access, through public boothsor telecenters which offer telephone andinternet services to affordable rates. As a generalrule, TV centers have had many difficulties in achievinguniversal access, for various reasons: expensive andunreliable Internet access by fixed-line and satellite connectivity, a small electricalsystem reliable, or a lack of commitment or ownership, for mention only a few. The adventof technologies wireless has opened up new,better opportunities for extend the offer of ICT accessand equitable access for poor. More and more options andneutrality solutions are being promoted technological change (such aspolitical measures deliberately not to favor anyparticular technology), including free standards, free hardware and free software, to encourage innovations atCommunity level. (For a more detailed analysis, seethe overview of the module Questions policies and regulations).

7.7.3 MOBILE TELEPHONY AND APPLICATIONS

Mobile communications, withmore than two billion subscribers planned for the end of 2008, have seen impressive growth inwhole world. In particular, they have been widely adopted indeveloping countries, with annual growth of 39% in Africa and 28% in Asia for theperiod 2006-2007. 45% of villages in sub Saharan

Africawere connected in 2006. The mobile phone has also becomethe most accessible form of Latin America and the Caribbean, which have seen their use go from four million in1995 to over 300 million ten years later. It is often theonly means Of communication which the poor have, althoughin most cases this Mobile penetration occurred in the absence of universal service or access.

Everything points to a modification of the economicmodel in the provision of telecommunications, whether provision of mobile more andmore flexible and costs more in more affordable or the obvious contribution of using pro-poor to the extension ofpenetration, despite the low returns from thesemarkets. The provision of However, mobile telecommunications requires performed according to the regulatory framework in place, and it is in the hands of private and / or public companies. This system prevents the viability of community property, but hasstill allowed pro-poor innovations for reduction mobile usage costs, with the popularity of prepaid, the ability to share amobile phone, the reminder the informal "sale" oftelephone services of mobile owners, the wide use of SMS, and many micro-financing projectsfor sellers of mobile. Here are some of the possible uses of mobile which have proved useful tothe poor:

The Grameen Village Telephone System in Bangladeshis

far the best known example. A

partnership between several institutions decides to try apopular company so

to offer its services to the poor. The model followed is that of a shared service targeting poor communities, with a microfinance institution (Grameen Bank) to finance the system, a mobile

company to offer its services of mobile telecommunications,

and a development institution (in this case, the Grameen Foundation) to facilitate relationsbetween the institutions.

A system ofvillage telephone operators currently operates in villageswhere there was previously no telecommunicationsservice. Phone rental allows you to pay loans andgenerate income. In Namibia, we see aninteresting combination old and new technologies,some newspapers offering free to print

SMS in separateinserts for those who do not have accessto the mobile phone.

In southern Africa, messageexchange systems such as the MXit (a GPRS / 3G technology)also experienced an immense success with young people, this technology allowingthem to chat with people at the computer or with other users MXit on their mobile, fromanywhere in the world, for the extremely small sum ofless than US $ 0.001

the minute. Today we offer a wide range ofservices

and applications poor communities, in areas asvaried

as the SMS information on the state of the market for farmers, mobile banking for the poor, or PDAs (PDAs)

to improve health services (seethe

Network case study

information on Mozambique's health). The examples

below illustrate the different possibilities offered by the applications:

A recent report on mobilebanking for poor (2006) describes howthey work in the Philippines

and offer banking services topeople without bank. By using this mobile technology between two networks of mobile, customers can now perform a number transactions, including receiving funds from abroad for reduced transaction costs. Given the low level of literacy required to use the mobile phones and the anonymity they afford to have,they have largely helped to mobilizeactivists for the rights human rights and democracy. So, an NGO for human rights hascreated a web portal that allows advocacy groups todevelop campaigns around their ownvideo films, most of which were filmed with mobilephones. There are also many cases of successfulcommunities fairer by reporting votingirregularities anonymously (Ghana), organizing events(Philippines and Ukraine), and denouncing corruption. Itis also possible to make a mix mobile phones and radio,as in the case of the project

Interactive Radio for Justice ofthe Democratic Republic of the Congo, in which locals can sendSMS anonymity to guests who aremembers of the Congolese government and United Nations, whichresponds to them duringprograms radio. The sending of SMS on mobilephones makes it possible to inform farmers and fishermen marketconditions and prices practiced, so that they are ableto determine for themselves when to sell their products andin which market. The Meraka Institute in SouthAfrica has been experimenting with offering mobile telephony in the field ofeducation, particularly for poor children who do not haveaccess to educational resources nor to the internet. They haverecently developed a mobile app which allows schoolchildren to send questions about their SMS projects. The systemaccesses the Wikipedia andreturns automatically the answers bySMS. Mobile phones are also increasingly used by NGOs for a mobile "activism", formany situations, for example in the case of emergency relief, for the protection of the environment, or for health service initiatives to ensure that medicationregimes be followed in the care of diseases such as tuberculosis and HIV / AIDS. Mobile penetration is veryimportant, but there is still many areas in which it is veryunlikely that mobile operators do not offerto offer their services, particularly in remote and sparsely populatedareas whose inhabitants are too poor to be able to pay highcommunication costs. He is likely that newcomers to the mobile sector also find these areas unattractive, and both centralized structures of necessary mobile networks(involving a top-down model with fewactors) that high costs installation are also problemsto solve.

The advent of new wireless technologies such as Wi-Fi and WiMAx, and the constructionof wireless networks by communities have created new opportunities to reach the poor rural areas.

7.7.4 TECHNOLOGIESWIRELESS

The most important technology package that has beendeveloped since the early 1990s is calledWifi, which consists of a wireless network platformbased on a standard international, 802.11, which works in the spectrum 2.4 **Ghz** to5 **Ghz**, and whose range is about150 meters. Originally meant operate in indoor environments using a spectrum without license, it allowed to install local networkswireless in buildings. At the end of 1990, the IEEE 802.11bastandard was

created to offer the possibilityof interoperability, thus allowing laptops and desktops to be networked without

require troublesome and expensive cables. This systemquickly has been expanded to be deployed outdoors, to allow computers to be wirelessly connected between buildings and over short distances. The fact that Wifi operatesaccording to free standards means that service providers are free tochoose which technologies and software theywant to deploy   for installation their networks,and that theyare not obliged to use software or proprietary equipment. Forpoor communities, this gives the possibility ofestablishing inexpensive networks with locally available and relativelylow cost technologies. Combining different technologies is also a way of give small actors a role to playon the telecommunications, allowingthem to offer services telephone and internet to local communities. However, in In many countries, regulatoryframeworks prohibit provision of these services, andaction must be taken advocacy to change things andallow the deployment of Wi-Fi networks.Two of the case studies analyzedin this project implementation module (the System Agrarian Information Center ofHuaral and the wireless network project of Nepal) illustrate how to exertpolitical pressure regulations may allow for theprovision of services to poor communities. In the case of Huaral, the Irrigation Committee, a local

community organizationassisting farmers, has been grantedpermission to offer services telecoms to its members, something previously forbidden. In the case of project in Nepal, the cost oflicense fees could be considerably reduced (from $ 2,000 to less than $ 2US), which has allowed community networks to offer affordable and more likely tobe economically viable.

Five years ago, a new standardwas created, IEEE 802.16, plus known as WiMAX, whichworks on a larger frequency band (between 2and 11 Ghz), which makes it possible to offer a broadband of better quality over greater distances, from 35 to 40 kilometers. Thistechnology is not yet very cheap, and is subject to regulatory restrictions in many countries. Wireless networks work formany projects and provide sustainable andaffordable access to communities, mainly because of their lowmaintenance requirements. ofthe enthusiastic specialists in wireless networks have also grouped online to help withtheir know-how. Next, examples illustrate the many ways to install wireless networks for community projects:

The distribution of drinking water in rural areas is an activity essential, now performedmanually in many

developing countries. A projecthas recently started in Malawi and in Tanzania to install a network of low-level wirelesssensors electricity consumption in order to control the quality ofwater in the villages. The goal is to trainprofessionals who can set up companies based on this technology. The Fantsuam Foundation inNigeria installed the first network without Community thread of the country, ZittNet. Following anevaluation on the However, she realized thatwomen used little this service. Fantsuam hopes to increase the participation of women in wireless services byabout 30% in 12 months. In South Africa, communitywireless mesh networks have been tested by means of"cantennes", to establish communications betweenschools, hospitals and communities.

Another project has placedseveral hundred Doors digital, open-source terminalsproviding access self-financed, in strategic public places of the communities poor, the system is maintainedby a member of the community. This self-financing systemallows users to access the internet and to differenttypes of content, such as Wikipedia. The business model is beingfinalized, thanks to brought by the National Ministry of Science and Technology in the framework of his supportfor the connection of evil communities served.

7.7.5 BUSINESS MODELS AND POSSIBILITIES OF COMMUNITY ICT PROJECTS

New technological options open up the field to

new business models that provide access

ICTs more economical for the poor. The obstacles of the start-up were reduced thanks to lower investments necessary, to the presence of information (and more and more studies case studies) on bottom-up approaches to network and access to ICT programs, thanks finally to the convergence of technologies that open the door to new more economical possibilities. In addition, the community international donor community are increasingly interested in community ownership modelsin the implementation of projects promoting ICT.

7.7.6 Community PropertyModels and Directed Models by the communities

Among the possible commitments, it may beimportant to involve the community itselfin a project. It is not a matter only for implementation in poor communities, since models also exist inprojects without relationship with development, and this type of model does apply not always necessarily to newsprojects ICT technologies.

How to get involved incommunity involvement:

Community participation by consultation : Most development projects believethat it is essential to foster active participation of communities in the differentstages of the implementation of a project. Great importance isgiven to participation and the contributions of the inhabitantsto ensure that

Project objectives areaccepted.

Community participation indecision-making : It is possible to involve communities at various stages of implementation implementation of the project,whether for conceptualization, planning, stewardship, orimplementation of large scale. They will own the project through agreements contractual arrangements withpartners who will take care of itself and will lead the project,or if they can take over when the projectends. This process involves that the community assumes varying degrees of direction andmanagement,

either through consensual mechanisms or by appointment a leader who will work closelywith partners to Implementation. Community ownership through autonomous initiativesand led by the community : Thecommunity itself the project and is responsible for the process as a whole. of the partnerships can be concludedat different levels (with the government, technical or financial support), and will beformal or not, bound by contract or bythe use of networks to access training, skills and know-how.

The level of Community control may vary: The contributions of the population according to theprinciple of contributions workforce, according to which the members wish to offer their time for the implementation of a project, whether by installation of equipment, construction of infrastructure, security of ICT equipment in the centers community involvement, or the contribution of volunteers to train other members of the community. Community management using decision-making processes culturally adapted, which can take the form of consultations with the main local leaders, setting up structures such as community forums, or the use of pre-existing or convened community structures especially, like women's groups or groups religious.

More formal management structures, including the creation of a hierarchical structure with employees (volunteers or not), setting up an administrative committee, committees consultative bodies, or local elected representatives, boundby contract to give strategic direction to the project. In the Huaral case study,the irrigation commissions composed of locally electedfarmers therefore belong to thiscategory. Community ownership through mechanisms such as

cooperatives (see section on cooperatives below), in which members or workersown shares and have voting rights for the project, in the same way as in the unions. New models led by thecommunity The ease of deployment andthe relative investments low requirements for wirelessvoice and data services

have allowed many experiments and feasibilitystudies to be conducted to determine ifit is possible to apply them in poor communities, allowing them to become owners and to maintain themthemselves or by

through partners. The casestudies of Huaral and Nepal are examples of community-led models in which the latter owns thestructures local communities (respectively irrigation commissions owned by farmers and schools). UNDP recently commissioneda series of studies on the feasibility of various community-led models in four East African countries. Thesestudies, collaborative ventures with governments, communities and local institutes research in Tanzania, Kenya,Rwanda and Uganda, present commercial projectsand cost estimates for installation and maintenance of community wireless networksthat include energy needs andcosts, a critical factor often neglected in implementation. These studiesindicate also the need for political andregulatory frameworks to learn about bottom-upapproaches conducted by communities in the provisionof telecom services in the underserved areas.

8. COOPERATIVES

Cooperatives have been around for a long time to respondto the cultural, economic and social needs of the communitiesit the construction of infrastructures such as electric or irrigation, purchaseof grain and equipment which benefits all farmers, orfor

political achievements as in thecase of trained cooperatives to fight apartheid in SouthAfrica.

It is usually in rural andremote communities that

telecom co-operatives areformed in financially attractive fortelecom operators traditional. Cooperatives havea crucial role to play in the contribution of ICTs topoor rural communities, and exist in only a few countries,they are very popular.

This model has been successfully adopted, particularlyin the United States, Argentina and Bolivia. In Poland, the cooperative model is slightly different since the Telecommunications Act of 1990 authorized the creation of 44 licenses in competition with the operator

state. In South Africa, special licenses are granted for

underserved areas (USALs). All were formed with the aim of developing fixed line, before the arrival of the mobile and the possibilities offered by

wireless networks. We find thefirst examples of ICT-based cooperatives fromthe late 1950s / early 1960s in rural areas of theUnited States and

Argentina, countries in which the deployment of infrastructure telecommunications has beenlargely achieved through rural cooperatives, through their financial contributions, theshared ownership, and the principle of personal contributions in hand-

 to put in place the common infrastructure for provision of telecommunication services. Number of these cooperatives still exist todayand continue to offer a wide choice of voice and dataservices to small communities underserved rural areas; it isalso the provision of multiple services that allowed them tosurvive. The success of their implementation work also depended on the creation of favorable agreements interconnection with incumbent telecom operatorsand / or sending subsidies, as in thecase of the United States. The most cooperatives started before the advent of telephony mobile, which has facilitated their ability to make them work.

8.8.1 MODELS DIRECTED BYTHE GOVERNMENT

Governments have led many initiatives addressing

pro-poor access to ICT, the best known of which is to create a universal service or an accessfund. Models followed vary, between grants allocateddirectly to concerned, subsidies to operators of tele-centers forensure a certain level of financial viability, or the grants and subsidies allocatedto operators of

telecommunications to buildan infrastructure for ICT in regions not governed bymarket forces. These

Public-private partnerships have for the most part been setup in following acquisition processes to establish pro-access poor.

8.8.2 MUNICIPAL BROADBAND NETWORKS

The recent establishment of municipal broadband networksis an interesting model in which the market does not participate and which consider broadband services the same as roads, as a common good. The developed world multiplies thistype initiatives, particularly in theUnited States where we see, forexample arise from the networks belonging to the residents ofbuildings and which charge themselves of their upkeep, as in Bristol, Virginia. In developing countries, theseinitiatives exist in particular in Knysna, South Africa, andwith the wireless network project of Nepal (see the case study ofthis resource kit). The arrival of these cheap wireless networks, sometimes combinedwith wireless fiber networks, canoffer competitive services communities that rival those ofbig cities. The Indian Government has evenmade statements that he wanted, with the funding ofthe Service Obligation Fund universal, offer free connectionto a broadband of 2 Mb of flow to the whole country. It isnot yet confirmed that these services are also offered in poor and remote.

8.8.3 PROVISION OF SERVICES TO COMMUNITIES

In addition to universal servicefunds, governments have made the choice to lead the delivery ofICT services in

communities, with or without external partners. In India by example, the government has undertaken various delivery actions services for the poor:

The wired village project inWarana was a project of online government to helpsugar cane growers, 50% funded by the nationalgovernment, 40% by the district, and 10% by the farmers' cooperatives of Warana. The project then integrated the Warana WirelessProject with the collaboration of Microsoft Research India, whichintegrates the original PC internet systeman SMS sending service by mobile phone in order to provide real-time access to theprices of market, repayment schedules, license applications and the yield of each caneproducer. According to evaluations, this system is successful, but it would be moreused by communities and they wouldbenefit more if there was a greater community participation, including womenand poor.

Lokvani is a public-private partnership program between the Stupor District Administration and the NationalCenter of computer science of India.

This project aims to provide government online socommunities can expose their grievances and raise petitions on the internet and / or SMS. The government Is a winner, sinceit can performance of national ministries, and citizens too, since they have so many channels at their disposal tomake hear their concerns.

In **Mozambique**, a project currently underway is trying to introduce handheld computers to service workers medical facilities in rural areas so that they can obtain medical information. This project is described in the casestudy on the Mozambican Medical Information Network (MHIN) of this resource kit, which is an example of a project Telehealth Government in partnership with the NGO AED-Satellite.

8.8.4 PRIVATE SECTOR MODELS AND CREATION OF COMMUNITY UNDERTAKINGS

Private sector shows growing interest in services

previously unnerved communities. Both the communities

poor than the private sector can benefit from many

services made possible by the improved range of wireless

low cost and other similar technologies, and the existence of social networks in local communities. This model is widely followed, in particular for banking and

many innovative applications for agricultural production, this to illustrate how communities can benefit

the private sector and its senseof organization, its experience market, its capital investments,but also a new range of services in communications and services. Mechanisms toimprove skills in community business, including mentoring systems, networks of skills support andtransfer of technical skills. Partnershipsbetween small businesses and communities also bring newopportunities for create models that benefit allparties, in which entrepreneurs bring their business skills to the table social development activities.here are some examples to illustrate possible applications of this model:

Cheap new technologies offernew ones opportunities for banking institutions in many development to serve isolatedand poor communities with "last mile" bankingservices. We see various models, ranging fromthe widespread use of mobile banking services in thePhilippines, to set up local agents serving as virtualbankers in communities. The models use on-air salesstructures, community businesses and mobile distribution, which are better structured and strongerthan those in the banking sector. These last mile banking initiativesthat make participate communitymembers represent new potential sources of revenuefor them through partnerships between the private sector andexisting community networks that cheap mobile phones andwireless technologies make it possible.

The well-known case of digital cabbages in India illustrates how can everyone benefit froma partnership between government, large private sector enterprise (ITC Ltd inIndia) and community. This internet-based initiative works since June 2000 and offersagricultural services to more than four million farmers from more than 40,000 villages, throughmore than 6,500 cabins that local farmers operate. The huge initial investment inICT infrastructure, especially in technologies suchas mobile devices or using alternative sources of energy, was provided by the private sector. Many ICT development projects are handicapped by the question of sustainability,which often leads to good concepts fail in their implementation.

More and more, we see partnerships be established between development projects community and local entrepreneurs. We can thusquote example of an innovative model from Soweto, South Africa, which

tries to implement laboratoriesin a sustainable way in disadvantaged schools. Alocal entrepreneur has

been responsible for openingthese laboratories, which use software free, to the community after school hours. The objective is to see if this model will generateenough revenue to interest companies, making more money at school. If that functioning, this model shouldbe replicated at national level.

9. RECOMMENDATIONS FOR SUCCEEDING IMPLEMENTATION OF A PROJECT

Mobilize communities andtheir

leaders in advocacy pro-poor policies and aregulatory environment

where there is none:

Regulatory Environments and policies have changed dramatically in recent years, and we're starting to separate the delivery of network servicesand that of their infrastructure,which modifies the role of theoperators traditional methods and pavesthe way for the provision of a wider choice of ICT services, which eachrequire policies and different regulations. The proprietary models are evolvingand including the actors involved,moving from the traditional model with a limited number of majortelecom operators, at an open model that plays a rolefor communities in the provision of ICT services. However, in many countries developing countries, it will take the help of pressure groupsto act on policies and regulations ifcommunities want benefit from the new convergence of technologies. Itwas the case both in Huaral (Peru)and Nepal, where they are groups pressure that has acted on thegovernment to remedy regulatory problems. It maytherefore be that communities must actively advocate and campaign awareness raising to acceleratechange in

 pro-poor policies and regulations. However, we notice some evolution towards theinclusion of new models in

international and regional debates, particularly followingthe success local models that makethemselves known internationally. Create services valued bycommunities: Projects will be viable from the momentthe community is starting to offerthese services itself. The

case studies where implementation has beensuccessful show that the involvement of the population in the implementation, whether by consultation by volunteers to determine which services would be most appropriate, or by creating new jobs for community members,has made a significant contribution the social viability of the project. It is also interesting touse community networks in placeto provide services to name of the government (for example, data collection medical, monitoring the stateof the environment, epidemiology, e-governmentservices) private sector (bankingservices, reserves for the harvesting of local agriculture or points ofdistribution of products and services as in the case of Digital Chupalsin India). Plan constant reinforcement ofkey skills Technical: Often projects thatoffer ICT skills to communitymembers see them leave for other projects or to the commercial sector as soon as acquisition of marketable skills. It is appropriate that the project provides for trainingprograms and reinforcement constant capacity to replacekey positions and ensure the viability of theproject in terms of human resources. Mobilize the community andkey stakeholders for get wide acceptance: It takestime to build a

relationship of trust, but the presence of a local leader is essential, be it a person or an institution. Of many examples of various applications demonstrate this.So, for the Huaral Valley irrigationproject in Peru (see the case study), the local irrigation committee took overthe project and has appropriatedit, so that he is a strong leader took it upon himself to adaptpolicies and regulations to enable communities to ownthe networks wirelessly and make them work as providers of telecommunications.

Establish technological viability: It is essential to choose a affordable technology, easymaintenance for

communities and use theresources now available networks of experts, particularly those interested in

setting up of wireless andmesh networks, as well as networks of resources like the MobileActive community. TheFeminist Technology Exchange (FTX)recently formed aims to form more women in technical aspectsand provides them with a informal support network. Itwould also be worth exploring yet alternative sources of energy to provide electricity required. Ensuring Financial Sustainability: Financial Sustainability of Projects small scale community andtheir objectives of development is often problematic. It is necessary tocreate financing mechanisms to ensure sustainability, which use especially :

Universal service funds (wherethey exist) and grants and / or infrastructuredeployment to assist in

provision of ICT services in underserved areas. Nil or very low interest rateloans, as in the case of model of rural cooperatives inthe United States.

Incorporation of the project through partnerships with others institutions, in order togenerate other sources of income, in particular access to credit through tradeunions or micro-financing (as in the caseof the telephony project village of Grameen).

Mechanisms for recoveringfunds for the provision of services tothe community, including:

Membership subscriptionMonthly contributions for users Rates according to use forservices rendered The labor input of communitymembers for install ICT networks andhardware

The use of volunteers for helpand training In-kind contributions such as the donation of buildings or

Computer Pooling community resourcesto obtain a

sufficient capital for thecreation of enterprises.

Demand for donations from the international public, as did the wireless network project in Nepal, which has put in place a system of dollar donations in partnershipwith a US university, which is another interestingmodel.

9.9.1 CAS^{2}E STUDIES

This module includes three case studies and provides a list of complementary resources. Project case studies are described below.

Project	Description Important	Points of the project
Network information on the health of Mozambique (MHIN)	Medical staff uses networks of mobile and handhelds to collect, transmit and manage Data medical, following the commitment of government to offer medical services affordable to communities	Users make part of the Staff medical and are the most often relatively older, and less open to the news technologies.

		Thanks to a training appropriate, they were able collect information
		And data in a domain that
		is
		helpful
		to
		population.
		The study case is about essential
		elements allow to do evolve a prototy

		pe in pilot project and to finally

		Succeed a sustainable deployment.

The system information agrarian valley of Huaral, Peru	The project provides telephone and internet access for poor farming communities and gives them access to an agrarian information system	The project provides access to the phone and to the internet for poor communities farmers and their gives access to a system information agrarian Originally intended for channel management irrigation using ICT for local farmers, the project evolved to also offer telecom services and internet access to communities poor who

		would have otherwise excluded of these resources

Nepal Wireless Network Project	Project of wireless networks from Nepal Wireless networks inexpensive and easy maintenance used in places isolated from Nepal for offer internet access and phone to communities dispersed and marginalizezed	The combination of a strong support from community and local leaders effective access to services of communication, Community and of companies requested. This study case is the example perfect of setting a project communal with few

resources

Other modules in this resourcekit present interesting case studies for theimplementation of projects at Community level:Business areas.

9.9.2 CONCLUSION

44 Since at least the last decade of the 20th$_e$ century, a break major impact has been made in the functioning of the economies and companies. Africa, despite the many problems that hinder its development, does not escape this rupture characterized by the importance of information and the technologies that convey it, in the occurrence ICT. These tools regularly shape our way of life, change the way we work, structure human activities. Certainly,

bytheir characteristics intrinsic, informationtechnology and communication do not lend themselves easily to direct measurements of yield and production, unlikeother sectors activity. For example, it ispossible to obtain results sof the influence of fertilizerproduction on yield agricultural; health expenditure on life expectancy,or even social and economic benefits ofthe investments made in the education sector. ICTs are not suitable for such analyzes of direct correlation with development. In Moreover, the impossibility of considering the observations made in the developed and emerging countries as indisputable iterations do not It

is also not possible to formulate a general theory on therole

of ICT in development.

Nevertheless, two fundamental ideas, from our point of view, help to perceive the dynamicand productive interaction between information and communication technologies and development. First, it must be admitted that the development is not only synonymous with progress innational income, nor is it

necessarily subordinated to this one. It is a much more comprehensive process thatconcerns

further improvement of theoverall living conditions of the human being (health,education, information, knowledge, etc.). In Consequently, the realizationof such a quest suggests taking consider all the factors that cancontribute to it. Now, on reflection,

information and communication technologies

contribute significantly today because of the context

new model based on the intangible socio-economic model information. Secondly, the factthat ICTs are not very suitable for direct calculationsof yield and production does not mean that they haveno impact on the

development. On the one hand,their effects on it manifest themselves generally much more indirectthan direct. Else On the other hand, currentmodels of development are shedding light on how toreconcile ICT and development through the roleplayed by information in the modern economy and society. In addition, the reality informs that these instrumentsare involved in most human activities wherethey turn out to be valuable development aids. In fact, everything depends on how, judicious or not, whose ICTs are associated with other factors of development, and the capacity or otherwise of populations, businesses, communities and states to use them intelligently in the routines of the economic and social order.

In all these respects, it can be stated with conviction that the term "ICT for development in Africa"

is not to be considered as a mere slogan of technocrats, nor like a lost searcher illusion. It reflects a reality which invites African States (despite their priorities development projects), businesses and communities in to make adequate investments in ICT. Indeed, these tools are in the process of forming in this 21e century a mighty development engine of nations,as it was agriculture then industry.

9.9.3 NOTES Rather, we favored a broadview of the subject (at the

African) because, in general, development (or underdevelopment), African countries do not

do not fundamentally distinguish one from another. It'sthe finding that we did through thetrips we had

the opportunity to perform in different countries of the continent. The problems are almost identical everywhere, to a few exceptions (especially SouthAfrica and the Maghreb in a lesser extent). Especiallywhen it comes to resources informational. For all that,most of the examples in the This study focuses on theIvorian context, which summarizes the African context, for the reasonsgiven. Jacques Bonjawo is an internationally renowned specialist of ICTs and developing countries. Computer engineer and

MBA graduate from George Washington University, he wassenior manager at Microsoft headquarters from 1997 to 2006. Adept of development through technology, Bonjawo had theprivilege of participate in major worldeconomic summits (Davos 2004, Lisbon 2007) for whichit was generally asked to accompany some Africanheads of state. Neoclassical theorist and Nobel economist in 1987, Robert Mr. Solow has studied the relationship between growth andprogress techniques. The Berkeley Round Table onInternational

Economy is considered as one of the world's leadingcenters of reflection and analysis of the economic revolution related to

information andcommunication.

Information is understood here in its broad sense; that is tosay, data (economic, financial andsocial); knowledge; entertaining and timely works.

Regarding the informal economy of the telephony sector Mobile Cell, an article of the author, published in 2008 in The **IEEE** Transactions on Professional CommunicationJournal, described the operating mechanism ofthis form of economy and especially analyzes its economic and social implications.Confer

IEEE Xplore Comsat (Communication Satellite Corporation)

is thename of the US company responsible for marketing the

services of the Intelsat satellite. Using the features of

the GPcombined with the system Geographic Information

Systems (GIS) and micro-informatics,

precision farming is an innovative concept of driving large farms. It aims at ensuringa production of quantity and quality whilelooking for the safeguarding of the environment.

Created in 1996, the RegionalStock Exchange (BRVM)

is a financial institution grouping the

eight countries ofthe Union West African Economic andMonetary Union (WAEMU): Benin, Burkina Faso, Ivory Coast,Guinea-Bissau, Mali, Niger, Senegal, Togo. Its head office is inAbidjan, Côte d'Ivoire, but central structures of the financial market are representedin

each Member State through a national exchange office

(ANB) linked to the headquarters by a satellite relaythat carries the stock market orders fairly.

The so-called electronic money transfer is so successful everywhere in Africa that regardless of the companies traditionally specialized in this activity (Western Union, Money Gram, Money Express, and recently Orange Money, in Mali which hasrecently opened hundreds of kiosks for the transfer money. A vast job creation campaign. They operate usually in partnership with banks or local posts), mobile operators have alsopositioned themselves on this very successful techno-commercial niche. The operators telephones also offer opportunities for younggraduates or

no by installing mobile phonesales booths and components. Installation and extension ofsmall and medium enterprises specialized in the field of computer science. Specialists in electronic, computer(networks, analysis, programming etc.) Africa needs personal computers (PCs) and laptops, fiber optic cables and cell phones to feed its technological revolution . Inother words, it is not enough the only technological systemto integrate the global "village". The businesses and public authorities must adapt to theusers

Who want phones that match their means, often

limited. Fixed phones have never reallybeen part of the landscape African . Operators gave up infront of the character inaccessible villages and thevastness of cities, and the lean income of the millions of families who live there, while ithas been so simple to mesh Europe and North America with cables from copper. African regulatory bodies Telecommunication Regulatory Bodies , which control the structure of the market and the dissemination ofnews technologies, are now part of the regulatory landscape world. Between 2000 and2007, the number of Africancountries to have with such an organizationincreased from 26 to 44.

Most of the investment from the

private sector, the

public authorities have the role of defining the basic objectives of their telecommunications policy; he returns to regulators to implement them, and it is up to

courts rather than other administrative guardians to ensure their respect. According to the ITU, 60 percent of African regulation are autonomous vis-à-vis the executive power and therefore independent ". Some experts are surprised that the creation of such bodies not triggered an increase in private investment. In America

Latin America and the Caribbean, private investment in

telecommunications increased from 13.7 billion USD in 1991 to 47.1

billion in 1998, beforedeclining for nine years, to reach 15.1 billion in 2007.

So it's the cell phone, which is brought everywhere and whose infrastructure are cheaper todeploy, which is the iron of launch of the Africanrevolution in

information and communication (ICT). Africa isthe only one continent to the world wherethe revenues of the telephone operators mobile operators exceed thoseof fixed-line operators. This is also where the penetration ofcell phones increases the faster. Governments have understood this well, drawingfrom new tax benefits. The inhabitants of the lost villages and crowded cities want ability to send short messages(SMS - short message service)

- "texting" - and talking on the phone - but without breaking thebank. The operators offer unlimitedroaming plans (roaming) from one country to another -a world first - and technologies adapted to the demand for online services, such as the bank distance or "cyber agriculture",which sees farmers find market prices on textmessages. Even the most modest findways to buy and use a cell phone - this is the lessonAfrica is giving us. But in this part of the world, Internet penetration

progresses much more slowlythan elsewhere and, in a way In general, access to ICT services is much less developed. This thematic of the PEA takesstock of the obstacles to ICT growth, listing the globaleconomic crisis, the lack of connectivity with the rest of the world, the inadequacy of regulations -which slows down the spread of innovative business models -and the problems of funding. Africa must acquirethe skills needed to innovation that alone can leadto a revolution

"African-style" electronics. The EU strategy defined in Lisbon sees the expenditure of research and development (**R & D**), structural reforms and a softening of the labor marketthe levers of a diffusion fast new technologies. But thisdiffusion also passes through better education,which is essential for accelerate the advent of the knowledge economy and revive the growth.

African countries have understood

that knowledge doesnot not only R & D. These are theinteractions between

local practices and traditionsand new technologies that, together, will give birth to newproducts and services, like remote banking.

Liberalization is for manyin this evolution. Big companies like Intel, Microsoft and Nokia havehired anthropologists to design new services, withpeople from the countryside.

As with developments in **OECD** countries and in the Americas Latin America, African programs for science, technologyand innovation (**STI**) are increasingly integrating **ICT**. The New Partnership forthe Development of Africa (**NEPAD**) is developing aprogram scientific and technological. The AU summit in 2007 asked for help from Unesco, and talks are under way with **OECD**, **Unesco** and the **WorldBank**. **Unesco** is financing a review of STI status in 20 countries. It also coordinates United Nations initiatives - through its group for science andtechnology technology - in support of **NEPAD**. Countries launch their own programs, sometimes with thehelp of international organizations.

Tanzania has thus developed a scientific and technological program with **Unesco** and the United Nations IndustrialDevelopment Organization (**UNIDO**). South Africa, Kenyaand Mozambique

also pursue ambitiousprograms. On their side, **Algeria**, **Botswana**, **Mauritius** and **Rwanda** have set themselvesas objective of becoming regional**ICT** hubs. For some advocates of scienceand technology, countries donors do not exert sufficientpressure for innovation policies . If they donot mention explicitly innovation, the **MDGs** recognize its importance by integrating indicators relating to access totechnology - such as the

number of fixed telephonelines, telephone subscribers mobile and Internet users.Most of the documents from Poverty Reduction StrategyPaper (**PRSP**) do not fully exploit newpolicies technologies and innovation,unless there is a real basis in their favor.

So in Ghana, thanks to thesupport of Kwame Nkrumah University Science and Technology (**KNUST**), innovation is included in the **PRSP**. If they all have **ICT** policies, the 47 countries that have reviewed in this edition of the PEA will need the support of the international community and the private sector to put them into artwork. Nepad is working in this direction, with its initiative on **STI** indicators in Africa (African Science, Technology and Innovation Indicators Initiative- **ASTII**).

The debate on technology in Africa must take into account the times the conditions to be fulfilled and the errors to beavoided:

ITS policies need to beintegrated into more extensive. Innovation and **ICTs**are not really part of

political priorities of the donor community. **PRSPs**

do not fully integrate the innovation, unless there is a real local support for him. Partners in need to strengthen national **ICT** policies in Africa ; Regulations need to be improved. Regulation by the state plays a key role in ICTsince most investment comes from theprivate sector. Too often, regulators favor the incumbentoperators of fixed telephony, which aregenerally unable to compared to new entrants - which hinders competition and discourages private investment. In contrast, manycountries have adopted best practices tofavor operators concerned, in the form of "convergent licensing" systems which offer more flexibility in the choice of technologies, and by

symmetric sharing of call termination charges. they have thus introduces more equity inthe regulations between fixed-line operators andmobile operators; Despite the financial crisis, the telecommunications sector in Africa remains very attractive.

The first available data

suggest that ICT investmentswill be less affected by the crisis in Africa than elsewhere,as was the case during the bursting of the Internet bubble in 2000-01. Several agreements were concluded at the end of 2008 and at the beginning of theyear 2009. That said, the prospectsfor new agreements seem less promising and investment spending is declining. The price competition is expected to intensify in the coming monthsand most multinational operatorswill reinforce their presence; New infrastructure linkingAfrica to the rest of the world will soon be operational. **Most network projects international** broadband Federer's aim to connect Africa to the rest of the world according to an open accessmodel. Rates of current wholesale prices - between $ 2,000 and $ 10,000 monthly megabit / second (**Mbps**) forfiber underwater cable **SAT-3** which runs along the west coast of Africa, and 3,000 and 5 USD 000 for a satellite connection - should start at at the end of 2009 to fallwithin a range of 500 and 1,000 USD per Mbps.

On the eastern coast, the first optical fiber submarine cables will be available at the thirdquarter of 2009. Five new submarine cable projects and two new satellite connection projects have been announced for the west coast. This work is supported by African private capital but alsopublic-private partnerships

(PPP) with internationalinvestors; Improving connectivity willnot be enough to touch more users. In addition tobetter frames Africa, Africa will need largeshared backbones on the continent. Retail priceswill also have to fall, to

like wholesale prices. Someexperts fear that fixed telephony operators inAfrica do not pass on the discounts on their customers, on the contrary counting on them to boost their revenue;in terms of regional

integration, backbone networks regional terrestrials are being built between main cities of southern and eastern Africa but also in landlocked countries of CentralAfrica. Algeria, Botswana, Mauritius and Rwanda plan tobecome regional hubs for ICT. Panafrican mobileoperators

provide free roaming services, making Africa the first region of the world tooffer this kind of innovation;

innovative business modelsprove that customers poor can be profitable. InAfrica, most mobile communications areprepaid. But the solution of micro-payment (less than 1 USD) to recharge an account is also very widespread. Ugandaand Rwanda have developed a microfinance business modeland the practice of sharing phones is common. SMS cancommunicate for less than a penny South African rand. Services funded by advertising are also verysuccessful in Africa. South.

As for new technologies and environmentally friendly energies, the environment, they enable operators to reach new territories; governments will have to privatize the last incumbent fixed-line operators since the essential know-how to upgrade their networks will come from private investors. This reform must go hand in hand

with a favorable regulatory environment for private investments in order to reverse the trend of the operators fixed telephony to lose ground regularly. The good ones innovative practices, such as convergent licensing technology-neutral and symmetric regulation

termination costs could help operators to fixed telephony to overcome their financial difficulties while establishing equal play with mobile operators; International cooperationpromotes technology and

innovation. Investments in telecommunications are more and more the fact ofcountries like Kuwait, SouthAfrica and Egypt. China supplies low-cost equipment and loans underfunded public operators.

For its part, India contributes to the constructionof a pan-African electronic network covering the continent's 53countries as part of a AU. American-style prepaidand expensive **SMS** Europeans are extremely popular. Cooperation on the e-commerce with the EU andthe United States takes a growing importance to meetthe regulations commercial. British and French companies have also heavily invested in telecommunications in

Africa. But South-North innovation could also work: Intel Class Mate ("classmate")computers, at a low cost, which were first sold inNigeria, are now available in Europe and the UnitedStates; New technologies makeadministration more effective public andbetter education quality; they also reduce thecost of business practice. An initiativeof Nepad aims to equip all primary andsecondary schools from Africa with computers, software and access to the Internet by 2025. OnlineBanking and Cyber agriculture, both of which relyon local practices, should reducethe costs of transaction and rebalance supply and demand on the

agricultural markets. /.

ABBREVIATIONS AND ACRONYMS

MFD	Multifunction Device
Driver	Pilot
CD	Compact disk
DVD	Digital Versalite Disc
ARPA	Advenced Research Project
INTERNET	Internatio rnatio

	nal Network
WWW	Word Wide WEB
UNESCO	The United Nations Educational, Scientific and Cultural Organization
CMC	Community Multimedia

		Center
USAID		United States Agency for International Development/Agence des États-Unis pour le développement international
CLIC		Local Comm

	unity
	Information Center
TIC	Information Technology and Communication
PTF	Technical and Financial Partnership
PIB	
COMSAT	Commun

	ication Satellite Corporation
SIG	Geography Information System
BRVM	Regional Stock Exchange
UNPD	United Nations Program for Devel

		opment
	ANB	National Stock Exchange Branch
	PC	Personal Computer
	IEEE	Institute of Electrical and Electronic Enginners

UIT	International Telecommunication Union
UA	African Union
PPP	Private Public Partner
KNUST	Kwamé Krouma of Sciences and Technonogy

ASTII African Science Technology and Innovation Initiative

ONUDI African Science Technology and Innovation Initiative

OCDE Organization for

	Economic Cooperation and Development
RD	Research and development
UEMOA	West African Economic and Monetary Union
ANB	National

Stock Exchange Antenna

Bibliography References cited

Ancarta, wikipedia...

Cheick Oumar TRAORE; Pilotsas agents of download in Mali; URLhttp //hdle.net / 186 610 316. Page

accessed November 16, 2013 Mike Jensen and Anriette

Esterhuysen. - Paris: UNESCO, 2001. - vi, 130 p. ; 30 cm. - (CI-2001 / WS / 2) Kayani, R .; Dymond, A. 1997.

Options for rural telecommunications development. World Bank, Washington, DC, United States. Technical Paper No. 359. Kayani, R.; Dymond, A. 1997. Options for rural telecommunications development. World Bank, Washington, DC, United States. Technical Paper No. 359. Khumalo, F. 1998. Preliminary evaluation of telecentre pilot

projects. International Telecommunication Union,Geneva, Swiss. Internet :www.itu.int/ITU-D-UniversalAccess / evaluation / usa.htm

Norrish, P. 1998. New ICTs andrural communities. In Richardson, D.; Paisley, L., eds. from, Thefirst mile of connectivity. United Nations Food andAgriculture Organization, Rome,

Italy. ITU (International Telecommunication Union).1998. Seminar on Multipurpose Community Telecentres, Dec. 7-9, Budapest, Hungary, ITU, Geneva, Switzerland.

USAID (United States Agencyfor International Development / United StatesAgency for Development international). 1996. Selecting performance indicators. USAID Center for Development Information and Evaluation,Washington, DC, United States. Performance Monitoring and Evaluation TIPS n °6, 4 pages.

Adam, L. 1996. Electronicnetworking for the research community in Ethiopia. In Bridge builders:

African experiences with information and

communication technology. National Research

Council, Washington, DC, USA,pages 123-140.

Anderson,; NOT, ; Pascual- Salcedo, M.1998 Community-led TV center planing stakeholder information baseline for Eastencap, Northem Cape and Northem Provence. CIET Africa; Universal Service Agency. Gauteng, SouthAfrica, 21 pages.

Evaluation of Télés centers communautaires. A guide for researchers Adam, L. 1996. Electronicnetworking for the researchcommunity in Ethiopia. In Bridge builders: African experiences withinformation and communication technology.National Research Council, Washington, DC, USA,pages 123-140. Allport, GW 1935.

Attitudes. InMurchison, C., eds. of, Handbook of social psychology. Clark UniversityPress, Worcester,

United Kingdom, pages 798-844.

Andersson, N.; Pascual-Salcedo, M. 1998. Community-led telecenter planning: stakeholder information baselinefor Eastern

Cape, Northern Cape and Northern Province. CIET Africa; Universal Service Agency, Gauteng, South Africa, 21 pages.fr.wikipedia.org/wiki/Microprocesseurfr.wikipedia.org/wiki/Périphérique_informatiques 1998. Telecentre research framework for Acacia. Report tothe Center for International DevelopmentResearch, Ottawa, ON, Canada. 66-page handout.Other books to read

World Bank. 1996. The WorldBank

Sourcebook. Bank World, Washington, DC, UnitedStates.

Blalock, HM 1972a. Causal inferences in non-experimental research. Norton, New York, NY, USA, 200 pages.1972b. Social statistics (2nd ed.). McGraw-Hill,New York, NY, United States.

Bryk, AS, eds. from 1983. Stakeholder-based evaluation. Jossey-Bass, San Francisco, CA,USA.

Campbell, DT; Stanley, JC 1963. Experimental and Quasi experimental designs for research. Rand McNally, Chicago,IL,

United States. CARE (Cooperative for American Relief Everywhere).1997. Monitoring and evaluation guidelines for MER users. CARE United States United; CARE Canada, Ottawa,ON, Canada. Management Tools for Development Organizations.

Chen, HT 1990. Theory-driven evaluations. Sage, Newbury Park, CA, United States. Covert, RW 1977. Guidelinesand criteria for constructing questionnaires. Evaluation Research Center, University ofVirginia,

Charlottesville, VA, UnitedStates. **IDRC** (International Development Research Center).

1997. Planning, monitoringand evaluation of program

performance: a resource book.

IDRC Evaluation Unit, IDRC, Ottawa, ON, Canada, 48 pages. Dugan, MA 1996. Participatoryand empowerment evaluation: lessons learned in training andtechnical assistance. In Fetterman,

DM; Kaftarian, SJ; Wandersman, A.,

eds. of, Empowerment evaluation: knowledge and tools for self-assessment and accountability. Sage, Thousand Oaks, CA, USA, pages 277-303.

Eichler, CH 1988. Nonsexist research methods: a practical guide. Allen and Unwin, Boston, MA, USA, 183 pages. Fetterman, DM; Kaftarian, SJ; Wandersman, A., eds. of, 1996. Empowerment evaluation: knowledge and tools for self-assessment and accountability. Sage, Thousand Oaks, CA, USA United, 411 pages. Fink, A .; Kosecoff, J. 1989. How to conduct surveys: a step-by-step guide. Sage, Newbury Park, CA, USA. Freeman, HE; Sandfur, GD; Rossi, PH 1989. Workbook for evaluation: a systematic approach.

Sage, Newbury Park, CA, USA United. Goldstein, H. 1979. The design and analysis of longitudinal studies. Academic Press, London, United Kingdom, 199 pages.

Gramlich, EM 1990. A guide to benefit-cost analysis (2nd ed.). Prentice Hall, Englewood Cliffs, NJ, USA.

Graves, FL 1992. The changingrole of nonrandomized research designs in assessment. In Hudson, J.; Mayne, J.; Thomlison, R., under the dir. of, Action-oriented evaluation in organizations:

Canadian practices. Wall and Emerson, Toronto, ON, Canada, pages 230-254. Guba, E.; Lincoln, Y. 1989. Fourth generation evaluation. Wise, Newbury Park, CA, USA. Henerson, ME; Morris, LL;

FitzGibbon, CT 1987. How to measure attitudes. Center for Study of Evaluation, University of California, Los Angeles, CA, USA; Sage, Newbury Park, CA United States, 185 pages. Henry, GT 1990. Practical sampling. Sage, Newbury Park, CA United States. Herman, JL; Morris, LL; FitzGibbon, CT 1987. Evaluator's handbook. Sage, Newbury Park, CA, USA, 159 pages. Hudson, J.; Mayne, J.; Thomlison, R., under the direction of, 1992. Action-oriented evaluation in organizations: Canadian practices. Wall and Emerson, Toronto, ON, Canada, 340 pages. Jackson, B. 1997. Designing projects and project evaluations using the logical framework approach. International Union for conservation of nature and its resources, Cambridge, United Kingdom. Kellogg

Foundation. 1998. WKKellogg Foundation evaluation handbook. Kellogg Foundation,Battle Creek, MI, USA, 110 Krueger, RA 1988. Focus groups: a practical guide forapplied research. Sage, Newbury Park,CA, USA.

Lewin, E. 1994. Evaluationmanual for SIDA. Swedish organization for international development, Stockholm, Sweden.

Love, AJ under the dir. from,1991. Evaluation methods sourcebook. Canadian Evaluation Society,Ottawa, ON, 213 pages. Marsden, D.; Oakley, P.; Pratt, B. 1994. Measuring the process:guidelines for evaluation of social development. Intrac Publications,

Oxford, United Kingdom. 175pages. Miles, MB; Huberman, AM 1994.

Qualitative data analysis:an expanded sourcebook (2nd ed.). Sage, Thousand Oaks, CA, USA United. Mohr, LB 1995. Impact analysis for program evaluation. Wise, Thousand Oaks, CA, USA, 311 pages. Morris, LL; FitzGibbon, CT; Freeman, ME 1987. How to communicate evaluation findings. Sage, Newbury Park, CA,USA United, 92 pages.

Morris, LL; FitzGibbon, CT;Lindheim, E. 1987. How to measure performance and use tests. Center for Study of Evaluation, University of California at Los Angeles; Sage, Newbury Park, CA United States, 163 pages. Narayan, D. 1995. Designing community based development. Social Policy and Resettlement Division, World Bank,

Washington,DC, United States, 55 pages.NRC (National Research Council [United States]). 1996. Bridge builders: African experiences with information and communication technology. Office of International Affairs, NRC;National Academy Press, Washington,DC, USA, 290 pages.

Parker, AR 1993. Anotherpoint of view: a manual on gender analysis training for grassrootsworkers. United Nations Development Fund for Women,

New York, NY, USA, 106 pages.

Patton, MQ 1982. Practical evaluation. Sage, London, United Kingdom United, 319 pages.

1990. Qualitative evaluation and research methods (2nd ed.). Sage,

Newbury Park, CA, USA.

Pfohl, J. 1986. Participatory evaluation: a user's guide. PACT, New York, NY, United States.

Rossi, PH; Freeman, HE 1993.

Evaluation: a systematic approach. Sage, Newbury Park, CA, USA. Schuman, H .; Presser, S. 1981.

Questions and answers in attitude surveys: experiments on question form, wording and context. Acadmic Press, New York, NY, USA, 370 pages. SPRA (Society for Participatory Research in Asia). 1994. Training

of trainers: a manual for participatory training methodology development (2nd ed.). SPRA, New Delhi, India. Stecher, BM; Davis, WA 1987.

How to focus an evaluation. Sage,

Newbury Park, CA, USA, 176 pages. Tardy, CH, eds. of, 1988. A handbook for the study of human communications: methods and instruments for observing, measuring and assessing communication processes. Ablex Publishing Corp., Norwood, NJ, USA, 407 pages. IUCN (International Union for the Conservation of Nature and its resources). 1997. An approach to assess progress towards sustainability. IUCN- International Evaluation Team of the Center Research for International Development, IUCN, Cambridge, United Kingdom. Tools and Training Series.

Valadez, J; Bamberger, M. 1994. Monitoring and social review programs in developing countries. EDI Development Studies, London, United Kingdom. Warwick, DP; Lininger, CA 1975. The sample survey: theory and driving range. McGraw-Hill, New York, NY, USA, 344 pages.

The Telecentre Cookbook for Africa:Recipes for self-

sustainability / Prepared by Mike Jensen and Anriette Esterhuysen.

- Paris:

UNESCO, 2001. - vi, 130 p. ; 30 cm. -(CI-2001 / WS / 2)

The organization

The International Development Research Center (IDRC) believes in a sustainable and equitable world.

IDRC funds researchers from developingcountries helping people in theSouth to find solutions adapted totheir problems. It maintains

information and exchange networks that enable Canadiansand Canadians to partners around the world toshare their knowledge, and thus improve theirdestiny.

http://www.idrc.ca/booking/index_e.cfm .

www.ingramcontent.com/pod-product-compliance
Lightning Source LLC
Chambersburg PA
CBHW060826220526
45466CB00003B/987